Women's Chronology

Women's Chronology

A HISTORY
OF WOMEN'S
ACHIEVEMENTS

VOLUME 2:
1850 to
Present

Peggy Saari, Tim & Susan Gall, Editors

U·X·L®
AN IMPRINT OF GALE

DETROIT · NEW YORK · TORONTO · LONDON

10/00

Women's Chronology: A History of Women's Achievements

Peggy Saari, and Tim and Susan B. Gall, Editors

Staff

Elizabeth Des Chenes, *U•X•L Developmental Editor*
Carol DeKane Nagel, *U•X•L Managing Editor*
Thomas L. Romig, *U•X•L Publisher*

Margaret Chamberlain, *Permissions Specialist*
Shalice Shah, *Permission Associate*

Shanna P. Heilveil, *Production Assistant*
Evi Seoud, *Assistant Production Manager*
Mary Beth Trimper, *Production Director*

Pamela A. E. Galbreath, *Senior Art Director*
Cynthia Baldwin, *Product Design Manager*

Linda Mahoney, *Typesetting*

Library of Congress Cataloging-in-Publication Data

Women's chronology: a history of women's achievements/
Timothy and Susan B. Gall and Peggy Saari, editors

p. cm.
Includes index.

Contents: v. 1. 4000 B.C-1849—v. 2. 1850-present

ISBN 0-7876-0660-X (set). ISBN 0-7876-0661-8 (vol. 1)

ISBN 0-7876-0662-6 (vol. 2)

1. Women—History—Chronology. 2. Chronology-Historical
I. Gall, Timothy L. II. Gall, Susan B. III. Saari, Peggy.
HQ1122.W67 1997
305.4'09—dc21 97-5028
[B] CIP

 ™ This book is printed on acid-free paper that meets the minimum requirements of American National Standard for Information Sciences– Permanence Paper for Printed Library Materials, ANSI Z39.48-1984.

Printed in the United States of America

10 9 8 7 6 5 4 3 2

Contents

Reader's Guide vii

Introduction ix

Photo Credits xix

Timeline xxi

Words to Know xxv

*Dr. Shirley Ann Jackson
(see entry dated 1973)*

Volume 1

Chronology: 4000 B.C.—A.D.1849 1

Cumulative Index 171

Volume 2

Chronology: 1850-present 181

Cumulative Index 353

Reader's Guide

Women's Chronology: A History of Women's Achievements explores the role women from all walks of life have played in shaping events and movements from antiquity to the present. International in scope, *Women's Chronology* entries each highlight a significant social, political, educational, or cultural milestone that has had an impact on history. Entrants—whether historical figures such as Cleopatra, scientists such as Nobel-laureate Marie Curie, or artists such as painter Faith Ringgold—were chosen both for their accomplishments and their lasting influence.

Women's Chronology entries are arranged chronologically by year. Sidebar boxes examine events and issues related to the topic, while more than 120 black-and-white illustrations help enliven and explain the text. Both volumes contain an historical overview, timeline of important events, "words to know" section, and cumulative index.

Queen Lilliuokalani of Hawaii (see entry dated 1893)

Acknowledgments

Special thanks are due for the invaluable comments and suggestions provided by U•X•L's women's books advisors:

Annette Haley, High School Librarian/Media Specialist at Grosse Ile High School in Grosse Ile, Michigan; Mary Ruthsdotter, Projects Director of the National Women's History Project; Francine Stampnitzky, Children's/Young Adult Librarian at the Elmont Public Library in Elmont, New York; and Ruth Ann Karlin Yeske, Librarian at North Middle School in Rapid City, South Dakota.

Added thanks go to Stephen Allison and Kelly Druckenbroad for their research assistance.

Comments and Suggestions

We welcome your comments and suggestions for future editions of *Women's Chronology*. Please write: Editor, *Women's Chronology,* U•X•L, 835 Penobscot Bldg., Detroit, Michigan, 48226-4094; call toll free: 1-800-347-4253; or fax: 313-961-6347.

Introduction

The Ancient World (4000 B.C.–A.D. 499)

Knowledge about women prior to recorded history is limited to a relatively small amount of archaeological evidence. This evidence was found on the European continent and is thought to date back nearly 26,000 years. A clearer picture of women starts to emerge after the beginning of the Bronze Age (4000 B.C.), when the earliest known human civilization was developed. These ancient people, called the Sumerians, formed agricultural settlements in the valleys of the Tigris and Euphrates rivers in Mesopotamia. In 3000 B.C. they devised the first written alphabet, known as cuneiform, leaving pieces of their history for future generations of scientists to unravel. Women figured prominently in Sumerian society. The Sumerians worshiped female deities, or goddesses, and the first known female poet was the Sumerian priestess Enheduanna. In Babylonia the Hammurabi Code (c. 1792–1750 B.C.) gave women economic independence and equal status with their

Georgia O'Keeffe (see entry dated 1920)

ix

husbands. They were allowed to own land and to pass their property on to their children.

Clay statues found in China and dating from 3000 B.C. indicate that the Chinese worshiped fertility goddesses. Ancient Chinese historians also referred to a "women's kingdom" that existed in southeastern Tibet during the prehistoric period. (Tibet, a region on the Asian continent, is located in southwestern China and borders India.) In this society women shared political power with male warriors. According to Greek legend, women warriors called Amazons ruled yet another kingdom in southwestern Tibet. By the time of recorded history Tibetan women had achieved equal status with men, including the freedom to divorce and to bear children without being married. Women and men shared property equally, and remarriage was common. Mahayana Buddhism, the Tibetan religion, considered the differences between men and women to be irrelevant. While Buddhist nuns could not study with monks, they did serve as advisors to nobles and government ministers, and many have been remembered for their spiritual accomplishments.

Considerably more evidence is available about women of the Egyptian empire (c. 2680-1000 B.C.). Pictures in Egyptian tombs portray aristocratic women as dancers, musicians, athletes, and priestesses. According to legal documents recovered from archaeological sites, women rented, owned, and inherited property, owned slaves, and sold goods. A queen, who was considered to have divine powers, was equal to a pharaoh (a male ruler), and the right to succeed the throne passed through the female line. Court women also helped promote scientific and cultural knowledge.

With the advent of Assyrian law between 1450 and 1250 B.C., women began losing their rights in the Middle East. Assyrian women had to wear veils in public, and they were strictly subordinated to (or under the authority of) their husbands. Similarly, women were considered inferior to men in Hebrew (Jewish) society. Limited to maintaining the home and instructing their children in Jewish traditions, women were not even allowed to worship alongside men in the synagogue; nor could they study the Talmud or Torah. Fathers had absolute authority over daughters, who later became the property of husbands. A Jewish woman could be divorced by her husband if she failed to bear children, but she herself had no right to divorce. Even though women were repressed in Jewish society, however, the Hebrew Bible contains stories of strong women who became leaders and judges.

Women had distinctly different positions in the two Greek states: Athens and Sparta. Most of the existing records of ancient Greece were left by the patriarchal (male-headed) Athenian upper class, which relegated women to a subservient position. Females were valued solely for their ability to have male children. Education was considered a privilege for Athenian women, and they were not allowed to participate in government or war. But there seem to have been exceptions, since some historical documents mention Athenian women who were scientists, philosophers, mathematicians, and teachers. Women enjoyed a small degree of independence in the religious sphere. They were free to become priestesses and join groups that worshiped the mother goddess Athena.

In Sparta women had more freedom. Their primary function was to give birth to warriors, so they were expected to undergo physical training in order to have strong children. Women lived apart from men and, if married, could be visited by their husbands only under cover of darkness, which was thought to increase desire and fertility. Spartan girls were educated along with boys and participated in athletic competitions. By 400 B.C. Spartan women had grown quite wealthy and were becoming conspicuous consumers. Whereas Athenian women could not own property, Spartan women owned a full two-thirds of the land in their city-state. Athenian commentators attributed Sparta's eventual decline to the influence of women in Spartan society.

Although Roman women were not segregated like some Athenian women, they were still defined by their membership in men's households: first the houses of their fathers and then the houses of their husbands. The chaste and virtuous (pure) wife was the ideal in Roman society. Because ancient Rome was almost constantly engaged in wars, many Roman noble-women became widows while they were in the prime of life. Scholars have speculated that this factor contributed to a rise in immorality among noblewomen. As the Roman nobility became fabulously wealthy and as the society absorbed the influence of eastern Hellenistic (Greek) culture, the rigid standards of morality in the Roman republic began to decline and ultimately collapsed.

After the centralization of state government began in India, the two highest Hindu classes gained power over the lower classes. As a result of the Laws of Manu, Indian women became totally subordinated to the adult males in their families. A woman had no role in choosing a husband, and she had no right to divorce—even though a man could readily rid himself of a wife who did not obey him. Women were unable to remarry if widowed, and for a time they even lacked property rights. Eventually, however, women were allowed to support themselves if they had no sons. Hindu law also established an unfathomable practice called *suttee,* or widow burning, which continued in India into the twentieth century.

Early Christianity and Islam (A.D. 30—1100)

In the early years of Christianity women took an active role in spreading the teachings of Jesus of Nazareth (Jesus Christ). While he was alive Jesus treated women as being equal to men, preaching directly to women and including them in stories to illustrate his views. After the crucifixion of Jesus (estimated to be the year A.D. 30), women became leaders and evangelists in the Christian church. The Roman empire almost immediately began trying to eradicate this new religion because it taught pacifism (an antiwar philosophy). By A.D. 400 more than 100,000 Christians had been persecuted by the Romans. Among them were women saints and martyrs (people who die for a cause to which they are strongly committed) who later became models of humility and strength in Christian literature.

When the Christian church was institutionalized, however, it was structured like a Jewish synagogue, having incorporated the patriarchal (male-centered) traditions of Greece and Rome. Women were once again subordinated to men. The New Testament promoted virginity as the ideal state for women—and as a means of controlling lust in men. Consequently many women became nuns and joined convents. After 400 B.C. monastic communities (houses for people who have taken religious vows, especially monks and nuns) were formed throughout Europe. Abbesses (female heads of convents) had significant power within the church for nearly 700 years. Nevertheless subordination of women in general remained a part of Christian doctrine for several centuries.

Islam was founded by the prophet Muhammad in the seventh century in an Arab region called Mecca. According to the Koran, the Muslim holy book, women were equal to men in their responsibilities to God. In Arab society at the time, however, women were still in a subservient position. Muhammad strove to improve the lives of women by outlawing the killing of female infants, allowing girls to be educated with boys, and giving more legal rights to married women. Nevertheless he held to the belief that wives should be obedient to their husbands and that single women were cursed (as were single men) and presented a threat to social order. Men took several wives, whom they could divorce for any reason. Men who violated (raped or otherwise assaulted) women were said to be punished in the afterlife, but unfaithful women were punished severely—usually by their husbands—on Earth. After Muhammad died in A.D. 632 women lost many of the rights they had gained. They could no longer worship in the mosque (the building used for worship by Muslims) and they could not travel alone on the annual pilgrimage to Mecca (the site to which pilgrims journeyed in the Islamic world). However, women did retain economic rights and remained dominant in the household.

The Middle Ages (A.D. 500—1600)

Historical documents provide more extensive information about the lives of women during the Middle Ages. In Europe most women were married as teenagers to men who were in their late twenties. Domestic life revolved around the institution of marriage, which was declared a sacrament by the Christian church. Only half of the women lived through the childbearing years, and nearly half of their children died in infancy. Girls served apprenticeships to tradesmen, and women participated in retail guilds, which gave them their own income and a protected craft. Many unmarried women were able to support themselves. In some countries women of the lower classes worked at the same jobs as men, but most working-class women assisted their husbands in one of several trades.

Women also played an important role in the arts during the Middle Ages. Noblewomen were educated in convents, where they learned to copy and decorate manuscripts. Nuns also ran prosperous workshops that produced some of the most beautifully illustrated manuscripts of the time. Another significant contribution of both noblewomen and nuns in the Middle Ages was the making of tapestries that commemorated religious and secular (or worldly) events. They also embroidered vestments and made panel paintings. Since the women usually worked in groups, the names of individual artists remain unknown. A few women even rose to the rank of scholar, producing books that provide valuable information about medieval life. Similarly, court ladies in Asian countries such as Japan and China became artists, writers, and performers.

In Europe, Asia, and Africa women of the royal class were prepared for ruling at an early age. Marriages for princesses were often arranged for political purposes at the time of the girl's birth; she was then educated along with her brothers to assume the responsibilities of power. Kings have traditionally been credited with major accomplishments in war and nation building, but many female regents and queens had long, productive reigns that contributed to the economic prosperity and cultural advancement of their countries. Throughout the Middle Ages certain women in European, Asian, and African countries became famous warriors, playing a significant role in defending or expanding their territories.

Near the end of the Middle Ages witchcraft hysteria swept across Europe, reaching the New England colonies in the seventeenth century. Although superstitions about heretical women (women who went against the teachings of the church) consorting with the devil had endured from ancient times, the Christian church—both Protestant and Catholic—started a witch-hunting campaign with women as their targets. In the late fifteenth century church authorities began printing hundreds of sensational tracts that gave instructions about how to identify witches. By the mid-sixteenth century people had become almost totally convinced of the power of witchcraft. Men were sometimes accused of practicing sorcery, but the main victims of witch-hunts were usually non-Christian lower-class widows who lived in rural areas. From 1480 until 1700 more than 100,000 people—75 percent of them women—were tried as witches, and a substantial number were executed.

The Early Modern World (1500—1799)

During the sixteenth century women of the working classes in Western Europe engaged in cottage industries, working for pay substantially lower than that of men. (Cottage industries are businesses comprised of laborers who work at home with their own equipment.) Nearly all women in the lower classes had little or no education, and they remained subservient to men. Educational opportunities for upper-class European women, however, began to increase with the Renaissance, the rebirth of classical learning.

The invention of the printing press also made more books available. Literacy among women was encouraged by Protestant churches so they could read the scriptures, and Catholic nuns founded religious orders for the education of girls. Women in wealthy families, who were taught by private tutors, became patrons (supporters) of great scholars; many engaged in scholarly pursuits themselves. Several women became well-known painters. In France ladies opened salons where the leading artists and intellectuals of the day discussed literature, science, and philosophy. These salons were instrumental in the development of the eighteenth-century Enlightenment movement, which promoted new systems of thought and art based on rationalism. (Rationalism is the reliance on reason and experience as the basis for truth.) As women engaged in intellectual pursuits such as composing novels and scientific treatises (written arguments on a given topic), debate about the place of women in society was rekindled.

In America women actively participated in the life of the emerging nation. Throughout the seventeenth-century English females as well as males signed contracts with colonists to work in the fields for four to seven years in exchange for passage to the New World. A few of the women married into wealthy families when they were freed, but most found servitude to be oppressive and their masters to be brutal. In the early eighteenth century the lifestyle of women depended on their class and race. By this time African American women had become integral to the economic success of many southern plantations. Wealthy white mistresses on these plantations oversaw as many as 20 household workers, a quarter of whom were indentured women. To the North, women among the middle and upper classes in the New England, Virginia, and Maryland colonies managed large estates and bought and sold land. Free-thinking women petitioned for the right to vote, many worked as doctors and lawyers, and several ran their own businesses. Some women in New England became writers and others were early advocates of education for all females.

The Industrialized World (1800—1899)

The Industrial Revolution (1750–1850) brought about profound social change in Europe, Britain, North America, and Asia. Throughout the world people were moving from rural areas to cities to work in factories and mills. Among those workers were women, who received low pay and labored long hours under poor conditions. At the same time, however, educational opportunities for middle-class women began to rise. In the United States coeducational schools were established in the early 1800s and teaching became the leading profession for women. As the level of education rose, women increased their involvement in social issues. Women abolitionists were instrumental in bringing an end to slavery during the American Civil War. In Western Europe, Britain, North America, and Japan, women campaigned for better conditions in factories and mills. By the end of the nineteenth century female activists were leading labor strikes, forming unions, and lobbying for labor reform laws. Women also established settlement houses for the poor, assisted in immigrant resettlement, founded philanthropic organizations, and trained nurses in improved hospital procedures.

An outgrowth of women's activism was the feminist movement, which began in the late 1840s and spread throughout the United States, Western Europe, Britain, and Japan. Women formed grass-roots organizations, held conventions, and lobbied governments in an effort to gain equality. They demanded equal legal status, property and inheritance rights, educational opportunities, and suffrage (the right to vote). Although feminists did not immediately win the vote, they were nevertheless instrumental in bringing about social and educational reform. By the end of the nineteenth century universal education was standard in nearly all the industrialized societies of the world. More and more women were attending college, and some entered professions previously open only to men, including law, medicine, and the sciences. Women were participating in the arts in greater numbers, becoming novelists, poets, painters, sculptors, dancers, singers, and musicians.

The Twentieth Century (1900–1997)

Women throughout the world remained at the forefront of social reform during the twentieth century, helping to gain new rights for themselves, for racial and ethnic minorities, for the underprivileged, and for the oppressed. During the early 1900s the suffragist movement intensified in all industrialized countries, reaching underdeveloped countries by mid-century. In the 1950s nearly every nation in the world had granted women the right to vote. Women's involvement in labor issues also continued into the twentieth century, as the world became increasingly industrialized. Intensifying work strikes and unionization efforts, they campaigned for the elimination of sweatshops, the outlawing of child labor, and the establishment of reasonable work hours. During World War I (1914-1918) women assisted in the war effort by volunteering as nurses, and when World

War II (1939-1945) broke out they replaced male workers in factories, businesses, and schools. Women continued to be active in pacifist (peace) movements during wars and conflicts since World War II, campaigning for an end to the draft in the 1960s and for nuclear disarmament in the 1970s through the 1990s.

Perhaps the most important development in the twentieth century was the "second wave" of feminism. Having begun in the nineteenth century, the women's movement reached a peak during civil rights and peace movements in the 1960s, particularly in the United States. By the 1980s women in Europe, Britain, North America, Asia, and some parts of Africa had gained access to most jobs, professions, and activities that had previously been the exclusive domain of men. Women were presidents, prime ministers, cabinet members, ambassadors, and members of governing bodies. They headed major corporations, led labor organizations, ran their own businesses, worked as stockbrokers, sold real estate, and managed factories. Women gained recognition as Nobel scientists, researchers, and inventors. They soared to new heights as athletes, astronauts, and explorers. Female participation increased dramatically in all areas of the arts as well, including film, theater, music, painting, and literature.

While women were still fighting political oppression in many parts of the world in the late 1990s, the gateways for female equality and advancement were opening wider than ever before in human history. And so the twentieth century will no doubt be remembered as "the women's century."

Photo Credits

Tz'u Hsi (see entry dated 1861)

The photographs appearing in *Women's Chronology: A History of Women's Achievements* were received from the following sources:

On the cover: Rosa Parks (**Courtesy of AP/Wide World Photos. Reproduced by permission.**); Mary Cassatt (**Courtesy of Archive Photos, Inc. Reproduced by permission.**); Nefertari (**Courtesy of Corbis-Bettmann. Reproduced by permission.**).

AP/Wide World Photos. Reproduced with permission.: pp. v, xi, 163, 208, 212, 224, 225, 229, 232, 238, 244, 249, 254, 257, 259, 260, 266, 268, 271, 273, 274, 275, 280, 282, 286, 291, 292, 296, 302, 305, 309, 320, 329, 332, 335, 338; **Corbis-Bettmann. Reproduced by permission.:** pp. vii, xix, xxv, 4, 6, 7, 11, 26, 34, 43, 64, 83, 84, 91, 131, 149, 157, 168, 186, 187, 199, 201, 253; **Archive Photos, Inc. Reproduced by permission.:** pp. xxi, 56, 166, 171, 205, 220, 231, 235, 263, 276, 307, 346, 351, 353; **UPI/ Corbis-Bettmann. Reproduced by permission.:** pp. 1, 93, 191, 213, 215, 223,

Women's Chronology: A Timeline of Events

4000-3500 B.C.   According to Sumerian legend, the goddess Tiamet created the universe.

2640 B.C.   Empress Si Long-shi originated silk-making in China.

c. 440 B.C.   Esther saved the Jews.

c. 69 B.C.   Egyptian queen Cleopatra was born.

A.D. 1137   Eleanor of Aquitaine inherited her father's lands.

A.D. 1429   Joan of Arc liberated Orleans, France, from English rule.

Eleanor of Aquitaine (see entry dated 1137)

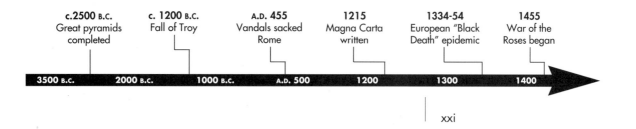

| c.2500 B.C.
Great pyramids
completed | c. 1200 B.C.
Fall of Troy | A.D. 455
Vandals sacked
Rome | 1215
Magna Carta
written | 1334-54
European "Black
Death" epidemic | 1455
War of the
Roses began |

| 3500 B.C. | 2000 B.C. | 1000 B.C. | A.D. 500 | 1200 | 1300 | 1400 |

1479 Queen Isabella began forming a united Spain.

1558 British Queen Elizabeth I took the throne.

1564 Maharanee Durgawati died at the Battle of Narhi.

1608 Midwife Louise Bourgeois wrote textbook on childbirth.

c. 1658 Marguerite Bourgeoys advanced religion and education in New France.

1677 Native American queen Cockacoeske endorsed the Treaty of Middle Plantation.

1691 Sor Juana Inés de la Cruz wrote an important feminist essay.

1718 Mary Montagu introduced smallpox vaccine to England.

c. 1720 Painter Rosalba Carriera introduced the use of pastels.

1762 Catherine the Great became ruler of Russia.

1837 Queen Victoria began ruling Great Britain.

1843 Sojourner Truth lectured about suffrage and abolition.

1848 The first "Woman's Rights Convention" was held in Seneca Falls, New York.

1852 Harriet Beecher Stowe wrote *Uncle Tom's Cabin.*

1854 Florence Nightingale introduced nursing innovations.

1856 Chinese "Dragon Empress" Cixi gained power.

1899 Senda Berenson wrote rules for women's basketball.

1905 Elizabeth Gurley Flynn cofounded the Industrial Workers of the World (IWW).

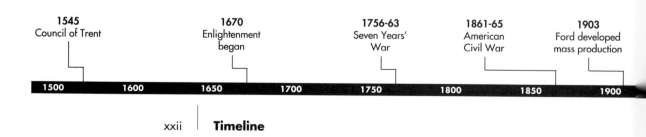

1545 Council of Trent	**1670** Enlightenment began	**1756-63** Seven Years' War	**1861-65** American Civil War	**1903** Ford developed mass production

| 1500 | 1600 | 1650 | 1700 | 1750 | 1800 | 1850 | 1900 |

1908 The International Olympic Committee gave official recognition to female athletes.

1912 Maria Montessori published *The Montessori Method*.

1913 Amy Lowell wrote Imagist verse.

1915 Lillian Gish appeared in the first modern film.

1924 Ichikawa Fusae led women's suffrage movement.

1925 Alice Evans pioneered milk pasteurization.

1927 Martha Graham founded dance company.

1932 Amelia Earhart flew across the Atlantic Ocean.

1935 Mary McLeod Bethune founded the National Council of Negro Women.

1938 Frances Moulton became bank president.

1940 Corrie ten Boom hid Jews from the Nazis.

1944 Hannah Senesh was executed.

1947 Anne Frank's diary published.

1949 Simone de Beauvoir published *The Second Sex*.

1950 Althea Gibson played in USLTA tournament.

1951 Marianne Moore won the Pulitzer Prize for poetry.

1952 Rosalind Franklin helped determine the structure of DNA.

1953 Queen Elizabeth II of England was crowned.

1955 Singer Marian Anderson appeared at the Metropolitan Opera.

1959 Ruth Handler created the Barbie Doll.

1962 Rachel Carson published *Silent Spring*.

1963 Katherine Graham took over the *Washington Post*.

1965 Jane Goodall founded chimpanzee research center.

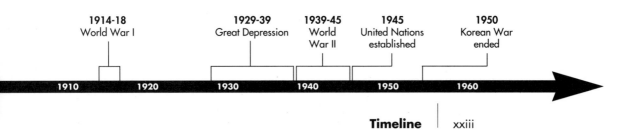

| 1914-18 World War I | 1929-39 Great Depression | 1939-45 World War II | 1945 United Nations established | 1950 Korean War ended |

1910   1920   1930   1940   1950   1960

1965	Opera star Maria Callas retired.
1969	Golda Meir was elected prime minister of Israel.
1972	Gloria Steinem cofounded *Ms.* magazine.
1975	Dr. Helen Caldicott led the antinuclear movement.
1979	National Women's Hall of Fame dedicated.
1979	Margaret Thatcher became British prime minister.
1981	Sandra Day O'Connor was appointed U.S. Supreme Court Justice.
1982	Russian cosmonaut Svetlanta Saviskaya walked in space.
1984	Indian prime minister Indira Gandhi was assassinated.
1985	Wilma P. Mankiller became chief of the Cherokee Nation.
1986	Chemist Susan Solomon explained the "hole" in the ozone layer.
1988	Benazir Bhutto was elected prime minister of Pakistan.
1991	Anita Hill testified about sexual harrassment in televised Senate hearings.
1993	Janet Reno became U.S. attorney general.
1996	Astronaut Shannon Lucid spent 188 days in space.
1997	Madeleine Albright became the first female U.S. Secretary of State.

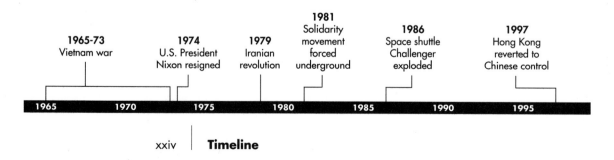

1965-73
Vietnam war

1974
U.S. President
Nixon resigned

1979
Iranian
revolution

1981
Solidarity
movement
forced
underground

1986
Space shuttle
Challenger
exploded

1997
Hong Kong
reverted to
Chinese control

1965   1970   1975   1980   1985   1990   1995

Words to Know

Billie Holiday (see entry dated 1946)

A

Abbess: A woman who heads a convent of nuns.

Abolitionist: A person who advocates putting an end to slavery.

Abstractionism: A form of art that provides little or no realistic detail.

Aeronautical engineer: An engineer who designs aircraft.

Anatomist: A scientist who studies the structure of organisms such as the human body.

Aristocracy: Government by a privileged class of people.

Astronomer: A person who makes observations of objects and matter outside the earth's atmosphere.

B

Bacteriologist: A scientist who studies bacteria and their relationship to medicine, industry, and agriculture.

Biochemist: A scientist who studies chemical compounds and processes in living organisms.

Biologist: A scientist who studies plant and animal life.

Biophysicist: A scientist who applies physics to biological problems.

Bishop: Supervisor over clergymen in a religious organization.

Bluestocking: A woman having literary or intellectual interests.

Buddhism: A religion that grew out of the teachings of Gautama Buddha, who stressed that suffering can be overcome by mental and moral self-purification.

C

Cardinal: An official who ranks next below the pope in the Roman Catholic Church.

Cartographer: A map maker.

Cathedral: A church where a bishop resides.

Choreographer: A person who creates dance movements.

Christianity: A religion derived from the teachings of Jesus Christ.

Cinematographer: A motion picture cameraperson.

Classical: Relating to the ancient Greek and Roman world.

Communism: A theory advocating the elimination of private property.

Concerto: A musical piece for one or more soloists and orchestra with three contrasting movements.

Conservative: A political philosophy based on tradition and social stability, stressing established institutions, and preferring gradual rather than abrupt change.

Convent: A community or house of nuns belonging to a religious order or congregation.

Courtesan: A prostitute who has wealthy or upper-class clients.

Crusades: Military expeditions undertaken by the Christian church from the eleventh through the thirteenth centuries to win the Holy Land from the Muslims.

D

Democracy: A form of government in which the supreme power is held by the people and administered through representation.

Dynasty A succession of rulers from the same family.

E

Enlightenment: A philosophic movement of the eighteenth century marked by a rejection of traditional social, religious, and political ideas in favor of reason.

Epidemiologist: A medical scientist who studies the number and distribution of cases of disease within a population.

Exile: Forced absence from one's country or home.

F

Feminist: A person who supports the political, economic, and social equality of the sexes.

G

Geneticist: A biologist who studies the genetic makeup of organisms.

Geophysicist: A scientist who studies the physical properties of the earth and its environment.

H

Hinduism: The dominant religion of India that emphasizes using mystical contemplation and self discipline to reach a state of peace.

I

Immunologist: A scientist who studies the immune system of the human body.

Impressionism: A type of painting popular in the late nineteenth century characterized by the use bright colors to simulate reflected light on natural objects.

Islam: The religious faith of Muslims based on the belief in Allah as the sole deity and in Muhammad as his prophet.

J

Judaism: A religion developed among the ancient Hebrews based on the belief in one God who revealed himself to Abraham, Moses, and the Hebrew prophets. Followers advocate a religious life in accordance with the Scriptures and rabbinical traditions.

L

Liberalism: A political philosophy based on a belief in progress, the freedom of the individual, and the need for protection of political and civil liberties .

Lithographer: A person who etches images on stone or metal for printing with ink.

M

Marine biologist: A scientist who studies living organisms in oceans and seas.

Matriarchy: A family, group, or state headed by a woman, with descendence and inheritance determined by the female line.

Medieval: Pertaining to the Middle Ages, the period of European history from about A.D. 500 to about 1500.

Monastery: A residence for monks who have taken religious vows.

Monk: A man who belongs to a religious order.

Mysticism: The belief that direct knowledge of God, spiritual truth, or ultimate reality can be attained through personal experience.

Mythology: Stories and legends about gods, demigods, and heroes of a particular people.

N

Naturalist: A scientist who studies nature; a field biologist.

Nazism: Political, social, and economic doctrines held and put into effect by the National Socialist German Workers' party of the Third German Reich (1933-1945) which advocated total state control of government and industry.

Neurobiologist: A scientist who studies the nervous system.

Neuroendocrinologist: A scientist who studies the interaction between the nervous system and the endocrine system.

Neuropsychologist: A scientist who studies the influence of the nervous system on behavior.

Nun: A woman who belongs to a religious order.

O

Ornithologist: A scientist who studies birds.

P

Pacifism: Opposition to war or violence as a means of settling disputes; also the refusal to bear arms on moral or religious grounds.

Pagan: A person who worships many gods.

Patriarchal: Social organization characterized by the supremacy of the father in the family or clan, with wives and children acting as dependents. In patriarchal groups, descent and inheritance are determined by the male line.

Pharaoh: A ruler—usually male—of ancient Egypt.

Physicist: A scientist who studies the interaction between energy and matter.

Pope: The bishop of Rome and the head of the Roman Catholic Church.

Prehistoric: Existing in a time before recorded history.

Priestess: a woman authorized to perform the sacred rites of a religion.

Primatologist: A scientist who studies apes, monkeys, and other animals such as lemurs.

Prime minister: The chief minister of a ruler or a state.

Psychologist: A scientist who studies the human mind and behavior.

R

Regent: A person who governs a kingdom in the place of sovereign who is a minor or who is absent or disabled.

Renaissance: The transition movement between medieval and modern times, beginning in Italy in the fourteenth century and lasting into the seventeenth century; a period marked by a revival of classical arts and literature and the beginnings of modern science.

Revolution: The violent overthrow of one government or ruler and the substitution of another by those who are governed.

Roman Catholicism: The faith, practice, and system of the ancient Christian church.

S

Saint: One who has been officially recognized by a religious group as being holy.

Salon: An assemblage of intellectuals, literary figures, artists, and statesmen in the home of a prominent hostess.

Shinto: The principal religion of Japan, Shinto is based on a devotion to nature-based deities (gods and goddesses) and worship of the emperor as the descendent of the Sun goddess.

Shrine: A place in which devotion is paid to a saint or deity.

Socialism: A political and economic theory advocating collective or governmental ownership and administration of the production and distribution of goods.

Suffrage: The right to vote.

Suffragette: A woman who advocates the right to vote for women.

T

Temperance: Advocacy of moderation in, or abstinence from, the use of alcoholic beverages.

W

Witchcraft: The use of magic or sorcery (power gained from the assistance or control of evil spirits).

Z

Zoologist: A biologist who studies and classifies animal life.

The Chronology

1850 ▪ Frances E. W. Harper began teaching career

Frances E. W. Harper (1825–1910) was born in Maryland to parents who were freed slaves. After being educated in her uncle's school, she started her teaching career in 1850 at the Union Seminary in Ohio, which was founded by the African Methodist Episcopal Church. Harper was the first female teacher at that institution. Moving to Philadelphia, Pennsylvania, in 1854, she was active in abolitionist (antislavery), temperance (a movement to outlaw or limit the use of liquor), and women's rights campaigns. That year she also published *Poems on Miscellaneous Subjects,* which had several reprintings and sold an impressive 12,000 copies. Harper later joined the Maine Anti-Slavery Society, becoming its first female orator (speaker). She returned to Philadelphia in 1857 and served as lecturer for the Pennsylvania Anti-Slavery Society. Her other published works include *The Martyr of Alabama and Other Poems* (1894) and the novels *Sketches of Southern Life* (1872) and *Iola Leroy; of Shadows Lifted* (1892).

Florence Nightingale introduced sanitation and discipline to military hospitals (see entry dated 1854).

1851 ▪ Su Sanniang participated in Taiping Rebellion

Su Sanniang was a rebel who participated in the Taiping Rebellion in China (1851–1865). As a traveling knight she roamed the countryside around Guilin in southwestern China. After avenging her husband's death (punishing his killers), she joined up with a group of Chinese rebels. Her military skill—and the remarkable fact that she defeated generals of the Qing dynasty (the ruling family that lasted from 1644 to 1911)—was celebrated in poetry.

1852 ▪ Susanna Moodie published *Roughing It in the Bush*

Susanna Strickland Moodie (1803–1885) was born in Bungay, Suffolk, England, the youngest child in a literary family. Along with her sister, Catherine Parr Traill, Moodie became one of Canada's most famous gentlewomen immigrants from the British Isles. She moved to Canada with her husband, Dunbar Moodie, in 1832, settling on a farm near Peterborough. Having published poems and stories in England, Moodie continued writing to supplement her husband's income. She wrote children's works and poetry, but she is best remembered for *Roughing It in the Bush,* which was published in 1852. In the book Moodie warned immigrants that Canada was not the paradise that it was said to be back in England. Her struggles as a pioneer and her mistrust of "Yankee influences" from America made her a legendary figure in Canada. Moodie also contributed to the *Literary Garland* and *The Victorian Magazine.*

1852 ▪ Harriet Beecher Stowe wrote *Uncle Tom's Cabin*

Harriet Beecher (1811–1896) was born in Litchfield, Connecticut. She had a strict religious upbringing and attended the Connecticut Female Seminary. In 1836 she married Calvin Ellis Stowe, a professor of theology, and moved with him to Maine 14 years later. Having published stories and short sketches in magazines since 1834, Stowe wrote her first novel, *Uncle Tom's Cabin,* in 1852. Neither she nor the public was really prepared for the immense popularity of this antislavery

National Dress Reform Association Established

The first organizational meeting of what became the National Dress Reform Association (NDRA) was held over two days in Homer, New York. Those in attendance at this first meeting—men and women from ten states—resolved that: "... in advocating Reform in Dress for Woman, our object is not to advocate for her positions of singularity [individuality, distinctiveness, or unusualness], eccentricity [oddness], immodesty [lack of conformity to socially acceptable ways], or to get her out of her "appropriate sphere' [in this case, the domestic sphere]; but to enable her to act with that freedom needful to find out what her 'appropriate sphere' is ... and, seeing a clear connection between her dress and her present condition, we are determined to discard a dress that is only adapted to 'womanly helplessness'" [meaning it was too restrictive to allow easy movement]. The NDRA, which survived until 1865, held annual dress reform conventions every year except for 1862. Membership, which was estimated at its height to include 6,000 to 8,000 women, was open to all men and women over the age of twelve.

work, which helped energize abolitionist activity among women in the United States, England, and around the world. An immediate best-seller, *Uncle Tom's Cabin* has remained in print continuously since 1852, with translations into more than 100 languages. Stowe continued to write, focusing on social issues. Among her other works are the antislavery novel *Dred* and the books *The Minister's Wooing* (1859) and *Lady Byron Vindicated* (1870).

1853 ▪ Emily Dickinson began secluded life

Emily Elizabeth Dickinson (1830–1886) was born in Amherst, Massachusetts. From the age of 23, after being educated at Amherst Academy and Mount Holyoke Female Seminary, she lived in seclusion at her family home. Dickinson spent her time writing poetry, and during her lifetime she produced over 1,000 poems. Only one or two were published while she was alive, but her sister, Lavinia, published three volumes after her death. In 1914 another volume, *The Single Hound,* was published, followed in 1945 by *Bolts of Melody.*

1854 ▪ Florence Nightingale introduced nursing innovations

Florence Nightingale (1820–1910) was born in Florence, Italy. After training as a nurse in Germany and France, she became the superintendent of a hospital for women in London in 1853. The following year the Crimean War (1854–1856; Britain and France v. Russia) broke out, leaving British soldiers dying from poor medical care, disease, and malnourishment. Nightingale volunteered to raise and equip a team of 38 nurses to care for British troops in Scutari, Albania. Introducing sanitation and discipline to the military hospital, she succeeded in drastically reducing the death rate. After the war, Nightingale returned to England a national heroine. She then devoted her energies to founding schools of nursing and a nursing corps. Nightingale challenged old superstitions and advocated such novel ideas as fresh air and sunshine, substantial nourishment, and friendly visitors to aid a patient's recuperation. She published the bestseller *Notes on Nursing* in 1859.

1857 ▪ Laskshmi Bai renounced alliance to Crown

Laskshmi Bai (c. 1820–1858) renounced her alliance (a bond between groups or nations with a common interest, usually solidified by a treaty) to Great Britain, the colonial power in India, and emerged as the Indian Mutiny's most competent military leader. (The Indian Mutiny of 1857 to 1859 was an uprising against British rule that led to years of bitterness between the two peoples.) Bai died leading her troops on June 17, 1858, during the Battle of Gwalior. She was often compared to France's Joan of Arc. (*Also see entry dated 1429: Joan of Arc liberated Orleans, France.*)

1858 ▪ Margaret Haughery established steam bakery

Margaret Gaffney Haughery (1813–1882) became the first woman to establish a steam bakery in the American South when she opened the D'Aquin Bakery in New Orleans. One of her innovations was packaged crackers, and her store quickly became the city's largest export business. She was remembered not only as a successful entrepreneur but as a generous philanthropist (supporter of organizations promoting human welfare) in New Orleans.

1859 ▪ George Eliot published first novel

Mary Ann (or Marian) Evans (1819–1880) was born in Warwickshire, England, the daughter of a land agent. After her mother's death in 1836, Evans took charge of the household. She was educated by tutors who taught her the German and Italian languages and music. When the family moved to Coventry in 1841, Evans became interested in philosophy and rejected her evangelical Christian religion. In 1851, after traveling in Europe with philosopher Robert Bray and his wife, she became a writer and then an editor for the *Westminster Review.* In the course of her work for this literary journal she met philosopher George Henry Lewes, with whom she lived from 1854 until his death in 1878.

In 1858 Evans published her first novel, *Adam Bede,* under the pen name George Eliot because she feared her work would not be accepted if she revealed her gender. By the time she published *The Mill on the Floss* in 1860, her true identity was known, but she continued to use her male pseudonym for her subsequent novels. Eliot's best-known works include *Silas Marner* (1861), *Middlemarch* (1872), and *Daniel Deronda* (1876). In her books she portrayed aspects of ordinary life and examined ordinary people—parsons, country girls, undistinguished scholars, and aristocrats. Her masterpiece, *Middlemarch,* criticized women's aspirations to be like men in their quest for money and a place in society. Although she never publicly supported the women's rights movement in England, she was admired by most feminists. The death of Lewes left Eliot grief-stricken and lonely. She wed John Cross in 1880 shortly before her own death.

1861 ▪ Tz'u Hsi became regent in China

Tz'u Hsi (1834–1908) was a consort (wife) of Chinese emperor Hsien Feng. After the death of both her husband and

In 1898 Tz'u Hsi supported the Boxer Rebellion, an unsuccessful movement to stamp out Western influence in China.

her only son, Tz'u named her infant nephew Kuang Hsu as the royal successor. In 1861, after Hsu attempted to institute reforms against her wishes, Tz'u took the reigns of government into her own hands. Most of Tz'u's rule was marked by a conservative tone and distrust of foreigners. In 1898 Tz'u supported the Boxer Rebellion (1898–1900), an unsuccessful movement to stamp out Western influence.

1862 ▪ Julia Ward Howe published "The Battle Hymn of the Republic"

Julia Ward (1819–1910) was born in New York City, the daughter of a wealthy banker. After marrying Samuel Gridley Howe, a reformer and educator of the blind, she became active in the suffragist (women's right to vote) and abolitionist (antislavery) movements. Howe then began her writing career, publishing poetry, travel books, and a play. In 1862 she wrote the "The Battle Hymn of the Republic," which was published in the *Atlantic Monthly* magazine. It became the theme song for the Union (northern) forces during the American Civil War (1861–1865). In 1868 she founded both the New England Woman Suffrage Association and the New England Women's Club. Howe also served as editor of *Woman's Journal* from 1870 to 1890. In 1908 she became the first woman elected to the American Academy of Arts and Letters.

1862 ▪ Kady Brownell marched with Union Army

When the First Rhode Island Regiment encamped in Maryland, Kady Brownell, wife of orderly sergeant Robert S. Brownell, resolved to be more than a water-carrier. When the company went to rifle practice, Kady accompanied them, practicing daily with her husband and others in the camp. She stood firm at the line of fire when a battle broke out, holding the colors (an identifying flag) and giving the men a rallying point (a point at which the scattered forces would come together). She courageously helped wounded soldiers and reenlisted with her husband in the Fifth Rhode Island Regiment. At the close of the Civil War (1861–1865), her discharge was signed by U.S. general A. E. Burnside.

1863 ▪ Mary Edwards Walker became Army surgeon

From her youth Mary Edwards Walker (1832–1919) was an advocate of women's rights and dress reform. In 1855 she began her career by receiving her physician's certificate from Syracuse Medical College. She then joined her doctor-husband, Albert Miller, in practice in New York State.

Walker was the first woman to be appointed a civilian contract surgeon (a doctor under contract for a specific duty and, often, period of time) in the U.S. Army, assigned to the 52nd Ohio Regiment during the Civil War (1861–1865). She adapted her fellow officers' uniform of pants, tunic, and heavy overcoat so that she could perform her duties more effectively. Walker was actually arrested several times in the years to follow for her style of dress. In 1865 she was relieved of her duties as contract surgeon for the Union Army. Her persistence in seeking a postwar commission, however, resulted in her being accorded the recognition of the Congressional Medal of Honor for Meritorious Service.

In 1917 Walker and 910 other recipients of the Congressional Medal of Honor lost their citations in a bureaucratic review. However, in 1976, Senate Resolution 569 reinstated Walker's medal, declaring her "a woman one hundred years ahead of her time [who] pursued many occupations including teaching, lecturing, and writing on women's rights, and campaigning for women's suffrage and other progressive reforms; . . . the only woman in the history of the United States to have ever received the Nation's highest award for valor."

Mary Edwards Walker was the first woman to be appointed a civilian surgeon in the U.S. Army.

1863 ▪ Olympia Brown became ordained minister

Olympia Brown (1835–1926) was born in Prairie Ronde, Michigan. After receiving her education at Antioch College and St. Lawrence University Theological School, she became the first woman ordained as a minister by full authority of a denomination (or religious organization), the Unitarian Church. Brown served congregations in Wisconsin, Massachusetts, and Connecticut for 21 years as a full-time pastor. Married to John Willis and the mother of two, Brown continued to use her maiden name. In 1892 she founded the Federal Suffrage Association to campaign for women's rights at the ballot box. She was president of the organization in 1920 when American women finally won the right to vote.

1864 ▪ Octavia Hill rented low-cost housing

Octavia Hill (1838–1912) was born in London, England. Her grandfather was physician and sanitary (health) reformer Thomas Southwood Smith. Hill was influenced by the Christian socialism views of theologian (a student of religion) Frederick Denison Maurice. When Hill was 13 she began teaching at her mother's school, and at 14 she managed a workshop for poor girls. She studied art with critic John Ruskin, who in 1864 loaned her money to buy slum houses, which she then rehabilitated for thousands of poor people in England. Hill not only rented low-cost apartments to the poor but also provided them with counseling. She felt that the poor needed to build their characters by learning frugality and thrift (how to make the most of their money). She also trained teams of rent collectors to teach middle-class household management skills to the poor.

Because of her success, the Church of England asked Hill to manage its properties, which eventually housed over 3,000 tenants. With Maurice, Hill cofounded the Central Council of the Charity Organization Society and the Royal Commission on the Poor Laws. She distrusted organized charity and emphasized solid personal relationships, businesslike practices, and self-help. A believer in natural beauty and recreation, Hill also helped to establish and preserve London's "green-belt" of parks and playgrounds.

1866 ▪ Ann Preston named dean of Women's Medical College

Ann Preston (1813–1872) was one of the first women doctors in the United States. In 1866 she was promoted from professor of physiology (the branch of biology that deals with life functions) and hygiene to the new position of dean at the Female Medical College of Pennsylvania in Philadelphia. As such, she was the first dean of the first women's medical college in the United States.

1867 ▪ Metta Victoria Fuller published detective novel

Metta Victoria Fuller (1831–?) was 13 when her writings appeared in print for the first time. In her teens she was known as the "Singing Sybil" for her poetry. She earned her living by writing in a variety of genres, including then-popular temperance tales such as *The Senator's Son* (1851) and *Fashionable Dissipation* (1853). In 1860 Fuller published *Maum Guinea,* an antislavery novel that was popular in England and the States, especially among Union soldiers. After her marriage to Orville Victor in 1856, she wrote "dime novels" (paperback dramas, often set in the West; Fuller signed many of these with pseudonyms, or pen names), and in 1867 she published *The Dead Letter*, the first detective novel by a woman.

1869 ▪ Actress Sarah Bernhardt achieved success

Sarah Bernhardt (1844–1923) was born Henriette Rosine Bernard in Paris, France. She enrolled in the Paris Conservatoire in 1859 and made her acting debut three years later. Receiving little notice, she took small roles until 1869, when she finally achieved success as Zanetto in *Le Passant,* a work by the dramatist Coppée. Bernhardt's fame brought her money, a new house, a crowd of influential friends and lovers, and more acting roles. She had triumph after triumph in such plays as *La Tosca, Hernani,* and *Phedre.* Bernhardt conquered London, England, in 1879, and outside of France she was best known for her performance in *Camille.* She made her first New York City appearance in 1880 and her last in 1918. In 1912 she appeared in the motion picture *Queen Elizabeth.* Three years later one of her legs was amputated, but she continued acting. When Bernhardt died in 1923 while rehearsing yet another play, 250,000 Parisians came to pay homage to the "Divine Sarah." Her writings include her autobiographical *Memories of My Life* (1907) and *Art of the Theater*, published a year after her death.

1869 ▪ Arabella Mansfield became lawyer

Arabella Aurelia Babb Mansfield (1846–1911) and her brother, who was three years her junior, attended Iowa Wesleyan University to study law and received their degrees in three years in a graduating class of three. Arabella, known as "Belle," was valedictorian (ranked first in the class) and her brother salutatorian (second in the class). Belle and her husband, John Mansfield, took the Iowa bar exam together in 1866. Although her husband was immediately admitted to the bar (meaning he was qualified to practice law), Belle was not. The reason was that the Iowa Code stated only that "any white male person" could be admitted.

Mansfield argued her own case before Judge Francis Springer, who made an interpretation of the statute language to mean that "the affirmative declaration [for males] is not a denial of the right of females." (In simple language, this means that just because the Iowa Code stated that men could be admitted, this didn't necessarily mean that women couldn't be admitted.) Therefore, in 1869, Mansfield became the first female lawyer to be admitted to the bar. It would be another three years before the statute was officially amended (changed) to specifically allow women to be admitted to the bar.

1869 ▪ Lucy Stone helped form the AWSA

The American Woman Suffrage Association—led by Lucy Stone, her husband Henry Blackwell, Julia Ward Howe, and others—sought suffrage (the vote) first for black males and then for women through amendments to state constitutions (not the U.S. Constitution). Five months earlier, the National Woman Suffrage Association—led by Elizabeth Cady Stanton and Susan B. Anthony—was formed.

c. 1870 ▪ Berthe Morisot exhibited paintings

Berthe Morisot (1841–1895) was the third daughter of Edme Tiburce Morisot and Marie-Josephine-Cornelie Thomas. She and her sisters were encouraged by their mother to study art. Since women were not admitted to state institutions of fine art in France at that time, the sisters received private lessons.

In 1868 Morisot met artist Édouard Manet and posed for his painting *Le Balcon*. Morisot joined Impressionists Manet, Claude Monet, and Auguste Renoir in their commitment to capturing the brightness and beauty of natural settings. Using everyday models, outdoor scenes, and less-than-realistic brushwork, the Impressionists were most concerned with the effect of light on their subjects. Morisot exhibited her paintings in seven of the eight Impressionist exhibitions during the 1870s and 1880s. In 1874 she married Eugène Manet, brother of Édouard and also a painter, and the couple had one child.

In 1870 Victoria Woodhull and her sister began a newspaper that was "run by female brains and hands."

1870 ▪ Margaret Knight invented grocery store bag

Margaret Knight (1838?–1914) was working in a paper bag factory in Springfield, Massachusetts, when she developed her first patent. It was for an attachment for bag-folding machines to create a square-bottom bag—the grocery store bag. Knight was awarded a total of 27 patents for such useful inventions as a window frame, a clasp for holding robes, and improvements to a shoe-cutting machine.

1870 ▪ Victoria Woodhull and Tennessee Claflin launched newspaper

Victoria Claflin Woodhull (1838–1927) and her sister Tennessee were daughters of an Ohio peddler (traveling salesperson) and his artist wife in Homer, Ohio. They grew up among theatrical troupes that included fortune-tellers and medicine men (healers). Victoria and Tennessee even performed their own spiritualist act (communicating with the spirits of the dead). In 1870 they began a newspaper called *Woodhull and Claflin's Weekly* that was "run by female brains and hands." Always controversial, the newspaper published the first English translation of the *Communist Manifesto,* written by nineteenth-century German philosophers Karl Marx and Friedrich Engels. (The *Manifesto* is a political treatise that discusses the principles of communism, a political and economic theory advocating the formation of a classless society through the communal—or group—ownership of all property.) Victoria Woodhull ran for president of the United States in 1872 and spoke on behalf of the National Woman Suffrage Association. The sisters also opened an office on Wall Street, becoming the first women to sell stocks and bonds.

1872 ▪ Author Higuchi Ichiyo was born

Higuchi Ichiyo (1872–1896), the first major woman writer in modern Japan, was born in 1872. In approximately 20 stories and more than 3,800 poems, she wrote about her own unfulfilled love and the unhappy, heavily restricted lives of Japanese women during the late nineteenth century.

1874 ▪ Mathematician Sofia Kovalevskaya earned doctorate

Sofia Vasilyevna Kovalevskaya (1850–1891) was born in Moscow, Russia. In 1868 she married Vladimir Kovalevsky in an arrangement whereby the groom gave the bride her freedom immediately after the ceremony. Such "fictitious marriages" were a common means for emancipated Russian women to avoid the severe restrictions placed on their movement at the time. Vladimir agreed to allow Sofia to study abroad, an ambition to which her traditional family objected. Although German universities did not admit female students, Kovalevskaya was able to study mathematics under German professors. In 1874 she was granted a doctorate in mathematics from the University of Göttingen, the first such degree awarded to a woman in modern times. Recognized for her pioneering work in differential equations, she was named to the faculty of the University of Stockholm in Sweden in 1884. Kovalevskaya also gained fame as a writer. Among her works are her autobiography, *A Russian Childhood* (1878); *The Nihilist Girl* (1890), a novella; and the novel *Vera Brantzova* (1895).

1875 ▪ Lydia Pinkham created patent medicine

Lydia Estes (1819–1883) was born in Lynn, Massachusetts. Trained as a teacher, she became involved in the temperance (restrictions on the sale and use of liquor) and abolition (antislavery) movements. In 1843 she married Isaac Pinkham. When her husband declared bankruptcy in 1875, she decided to combat poverty by selling an herbal mixture she called "Lydia E. Pinkham's Vegetable Compound." Although the mixture had no evident curative powers, its bright blue label claimed it would cure all female weaknesses. The product became the best-known patent medicine in the United States, earning Pinkham fame and prosperity. She became the first woman to establish her reputation by selling medicine.

1876 ▪ Lilli Lehmann premiered Wagner role

Lilli Lehmann (1848–1929) was born in Würzburg, Germany. Trained as a singer by her mother in Prague, Czechoslovakia, she made her debut in *The Magic Flute,* an opera by Austrian composer Wolfgang Amadeus Mozart. Eventually mastering 170 roles, she sang primarily in Berlin, Germany, and New York City. Lehmann became internationally known for her roles in operas by famed German composer Richard Wagner. In 1876 she appeared in the first performance of *Ring des Nibelungen* at Bayreuth, a center for the performance of works by Wagner. Lehmann was instrumental in founding opera festivals in Salzburg, Austria; Danzig (also called

---

Women Are Denied the Vote

Susan B. Anthony and 15 other women were arrested in Rochester, New York, for attempting to vote in the 1872 presidential election. (Anthony wanted to cast her vote for Ulysses S. Grant.) Anthony was arrested and fined 100 dollars, which she refused to pay. African American orator Sojourner Truth demanded a ballot in Grand Rapids, Michigan, but she was denied the right to vote as well.

Gdansk, a city and port in northern Poland); Leipzig, Germany; and London, England. Lehmann starred in the premiere of Wagner's *Tristan and Isolde* at the Metropolitan Opera House in New York City.

1876 ▪ Painter Paula Modersohn-Becker was born

Paula Modersohn-Becker (1876–1907) is remembered as a significant German artist. Modersohn-Becker, who died after childbirth, is currently regarded as one of the most powerful figure painters of the twentieth century. During her lifetime, however, her work was considered crude and shocking. She was noted for her still lifes, self-portraits, and pictures of mothers and children, all of which exemplified her naturalistic style in broad areas of color.

1876 ▪ Hubertine Auclert became leading French suffragist

Hubertine Auclert (1848–1914) was a leading French suffragist (fighter for women's right to vote) during the late 1800s. In 1876 she formed the Society for Women's Rights, which she renamed the Society for Women's Suffrage in 1883 to better reflect its goal. From 1881 to 1891 she published *The Citizen,* a newspaper dedicated to female suffrage. In 1888 she married Antonin Levier and moved with him to Algeria (a country in northwestern Africa), where they lived until his death four years later. Auclert died in 1914 without seeing women gain the vote.

1879 ▪ Frances Willard headed WCTU

Frances Willard (1839–1898) was born in Churchville, New York. After completing her studies at Northwestern Female College in Illinois, she stayed on as a member of the faculty. Playing an important role in education for women in Illinois, she later was president and dean of the college before it merged with Northwestern University. In 1879 Willard became president of the Women's Christian Temperance Union (WCTU), which was established in 1874 to end the sale and consumption of alcohol. Willard believed that giving women the right to vote would more than likely cure society's major ills. Under her leadership the WCTU became the largest women's organization in the United States by 1880. A statue of Willard represents the state of Illinois in Statuary Hall in the U.S. Capitol in Washington, D.C.

1881 ▪ Activist Sofia Perovskaya was executed

Sofia Perovskaya (1854–1881) was born in Russia. Rebelling against her father's conservatism (a tendency to reject change and hold on to traditional beliefs), she became active in radical politics in the 1860s and 1870s through lecture courses and discussion groups in St. Petersburg. Perovskaya became an passionate advocate of women's rights and social reform in tsarist (monarchist; headed by a royal family) Russia. Engaged in spreading antigovernment propaganda among the peasants in the countryside, she was forced into an underground existence in the mid–1870s. Finally, Perovskaya joined the People's Will, a terrorist group planning to kill Tsar Alexander II. She took a leading part in three assassination attempts, the third being successful in 1881. Shortly thereafter Perovskaya was hanged—along with three men—making her the first Russian woman to be executed for a political crime. As a result of Perovskaya's actions, in 1876 women were banned from entering Russian universities. The ban was not lifted until 1905.

1881 ▪ Elizabeth Bagshaw pioneered birth control

Elizabeth Bagshaw was born near Cannington, Ontario, Canada. She practiced medicine for 60 years, but she was best known for her 30 years as the medical director of the Hamilton Birth Control Clinic, which she opened in 1881. While "rising relief costs" (welfare costs) caused her great concern, her main motivation was concern for the plight of working-class women who faced repeated unwanted pregnancies. Founded and financed by a wealthy widow, the clinic often distributed contraceptives (birth control devices) free of charge. Despite opposition from medical colleagues and local clergy, Bagshaw continued to work with volunteers to promote inexpensive and reliable contraception. She received many honors throughout her life, including an honorary doctorate from McMaster University in Hamilton, Ontario.

1882 ▪ Kishida Toshiko attacked negative attitudes

Kishida Toshiko (c. 1863–1901) was born in Japan. Because she excelled in her study of the Chinese and Japanese classics, she became the first commoner to serve as a lady-in-waiting to an empress—the empress Shoken (1850–1914). Toshiko left court in 1882, however, to embark on a national lecture tour, sponsored by the Jiyuto (Liberal Party). In her lectures she spoke of women as participants in the establishment of a new Japanese society. Toshiko attacked the Confucian (established by the ancient Chinese philosopher Confucius) "three obediences," whereby women were kept under the control of their fathers, husbands, or sons throughout their lives.

She criticized the marriage system, which did not allow divorce, and the concubine system, which permitted men to keep numerous women as mistresses. Toshiko also campaigned for better educational opportunities for girls. She encouraged women to organize discussion groups and lecture societies as a means of promoting equal rights. The Peace Preservation Law of 1887, which prohibited women from engaging in political activities, effectively ended her speaking career. (It is thought that Toshiko, in particular, was meant to be the target of this legislation.) However, Toshiko continued to contribute poems and essays to the periodical *Jogaku Zasshi* and was said to have made a fortune in real estate dealings.

1884 ▪ Kate Gleason studied engineering

Kate Gleason (1865–1933) was the first woman to register to study mechanical engineering in the United States. She attended classes at Cornell University from 1884 to 1889. Although she never obtained a degree, she practiced engineering for many years at her father's firm, Gleason Machine Tools Company. Winning renown for her original design of worm gears, she helped the company to become the leading manufacturer of specialized gears.

1885 ▪ Annie Oakley gained fame as sharpshooter

Phoebe Anne Mosey (1860–1926), later known as Annie Oakley, was born in Ohio to a Quaker family. As a young girl she learned to shoot in order to provide food for her family. Eventually she sold the game (wild birds and animals), and she did so well in the Cincinnati market that she was able to pay off the family farm mortgage. In 1880 she married vaudeville marksman Frank Butler after beating him in a shooting match. Five years later she joined Buffalo Bill's Wild West show as a sharpshooter, remaining one of the star attractions for 17 years. Oakley's story was the basis of two films and a play.

1886 ▪ Journalist Sara Jeanette Duncan started career

Sara Jeanette Duncan (1861–1922) was born in Brantford, Ontario, Canada. During the 1880s Duncan became the first woman employed full-time by the *Toronto Globe* (1886–1887) and then by the *Montreal Star* (1887–1888). She also wrote for other newspapers under the pseudonym Garth Grafton. After taking a round-the-world trip (1888–1890), she turned to writing books. Among her novels are *The Imperialist* and *Cousin Cinderella,* which presented brilliant studies of social attitudes in contemporary Canadian society. Duncan was married to Everard Cotes, a museum curator in Calcutta, India, where the couple lived for 25 years. Her novel *The Simple Adventures of a Memsahib* (1893) is set in India.

1887 ▪ Alexandra Gripenberg supported feminism

Alexandra Gripenberg (1857–1911) was the well-educated daughter of a Finnish senator and baron. In 1887 she decided to devote her energy to the feminist (women's rights) movement in Finland, serving as president of the Finnish Women's Association for 20 years. When women's suffrage (the right to vote) was introduced in Finland in 1906, Gripenberg was elected to the national assembly. She wrote a history of the feminist movement in both the Finnish and Swedish languages.

1888 ▪ Leonora Barry elected to Knights of Labor

Leonora Barry (1849–1930) was born in County Cork, Ireland. In 1852 she immigrated to the United States and worked in a clothing factory. Thirty-six years later she was elected master workman—the highest position a woman could hold—at the national Knights of Labor convention.

Barry headed a district assembly of nearly 1,000 women Knights of Labor in upstate New York. At the same convention the Knights became the first labor organization to establish a department of women's work and appointed Barry as its first general investigator. In that capacity she organized new assemblies, traveled extensively (an unheard-of act for a woman alone during that time), and answered hundreds of letters, telegrams, and other requests for help from women workers. In reports to the annual conventions of 1887, 1888, and 1889 Barry presented the first nationwide statistics on women workers. She faced considerable opposition to her efforts. Male Knights criticized her, and many Catholic priests of the day denounced her as a "lady tramp" because she traveled, spoke publicly, and encouraged women to organize and join unions.

1888 ▪ Susan B. Anthony organized International Council of Women

In 1888 American reformer Susan B. Anthony organized the International Council of Women with representatives from 48 countries. She was elected to the American Hall of Fame in 1950. The U.S. government issued a one-dollar Susan B. Anthony coin in 1979, making her the first U.S. woman to have her likeness on a coin in general circulation.

1890 ▪ Nellie Bly set around-the-world travel record

Nellie Bly was the pseudonym of Elizabeth Cochrane Seaman (1865–1922), who was born in Cochran's Mills, Pennsylvania. Seaman adopted her pen name from a popular song while she was a reporter for the *Pittsburgh Dispatch* newspaper, where she wrote on reform issues and then-controversial topics such as divorce. After moving to New York City she worked for the *World* newspaper as a writer of exposés of poor conditions for workers and in women's prisons. Bly is best known for beating the 80-day around-the-world record set by the fictional Phineas Fogg in French writer Jules Verne's *Around the World in Eighty Days. The World* sent her on the mission, which she accomplished traveling by train, handcar, ship, and burro. Bly sailed from Hoboken, New Jersey, on November 14, 1889, and arrived on January 25, 1890, 72 days later by train in New York City. Her front-page stories in the *World* were widely read. Bly wrote about her experiences on the excursion in *Nelly Bly's Book: Around the World in Seventy-Two Days.*

Sharpshooters Calamity Jane and Annie Oakley (above) were both featured performers in Buffalo Bill's Wild West Show.

1891 ▪ Calamity Jane joined Buffalo Bill's Wild West Show

Martha Jane Cannary Burke (1852–1903), known as "Calamity Jane," was born in Princeton, Missouri. As a girl she acquired the skills of riding and shooting. Around 1876 she became involved with U.S. marshal Wild Bill Hickok, who was murdered later that year. Afterward she claimed he was the father of a child she had in 1873. During a smallpox epidemic in Deadwood, South Dakota, she disguised herself as a man and nursed victims of the disease. She is said to have earned her nickname by threatening "calamity" (trouble) to any man who wanted to marry her. Nevertheless, in 1891 she married Clinton Burke, with whom she had been living for six years. After she and her husband parted she became the first woman to perform in Buffalo Bill's Wild West Show as it traveled throughout America. She also appeared with Buffalo Bill when he took his show to England in 1893. Jane was fired from the 1901 Pan-American Exposition in Buffalo, New York, for being drunk and offensive.

1891 ▪ Psychologist Mary Calkins founded laboratory

Mary Whiton Calkins (1863–1930) was an American psychologist and philosopher. After earning a degree from Smith College with a concentration in the classics, Calkins began teaching Greek at Wellesley College in 1887. In 1888 she was offered the new position of instructor in psychology, provided she had a year's training in the discipline. Consistent with university policy toward women in 1890, Calkins was granted special permission to attend classes in psychology and philosophy at Harvard University and in laboratory psychology at Clark University in Worcester, Massachusetts. She was denied admission to their graduate studies programs, though, and she was also denied permission to attend regular Harvard seminars. Finally Harvard faculty members William James and Josiah Royce, as well as Calkins's father, intervened on her behalf.

Returning to Wellesley in the fall of 1891 Calkins established the first psychology laboratory at a women's college in the United States. In 1895 Calkins requested and took an examination equivalent to the official Ph.D. exam. Her performance was praised by James as "the most brilliant examination for the Ph.D. that we have had at Harvard." Nevertheless, Calkins was still denied admission to candidacy for the degree.

With the creation of Radcliffe College in 1902, Calkins was one of the first four women to be offered the Ph.D., but she refused it in protest. In 1905 she became the first woman president of the American Psychological Association, and 1918 she was the first woman president of the American Philosophical Association. Calkins taught at Wellesley College until her retirement in 1929 and published four books and more than 100 papers in psychology and philosophy.

1892 ▪ Sophia Haydn designed "Women's Building"

Sophia Haydn (1869–1953) was the first woman to graduate in architecture from the Massachusetts Institute of Technology (MIT) in Cambridge, Massachusetts. She won the competition to design the Women's Building at the 1892–1893 World's Columbian Exposition in Chicago. The exposition commemorated the four hundredth anniversary of Christopher Columbus's discovery of America. Haydn's design was for an Italian Renaissance exhibit hall with skylights. Devastated by the pressure of supervising such a large construction project and stung by the negative critical response to her work, Haydn never designed another building.

1892 ▪ Ida B. Wells Barnett published *Southern Horrors*

Ida B. Wells Barnett (1862–1931) was born in Holly Springs, Mississippi, the daughter of former slaves. After teaching school for a time, she became a journalist in Memphis, Tennessee. Using the pen name "Iola," she wrote articles for African American newspapers. While working as a reporter, Wells Barnett became active in civil rights causes, including a campaign against the lynching of blacks by whites. She published *Southern Horrors,* a pamphlet about the crimes, in 1892. In 1895 she married Ferdinand Lee Barnett, a Chicago newspaper editor. After moving to Chicago, Wells Barnett was one of two women who signed the proposal for the formation of the National Association for the Advancement of Colored People (NAACP). She also founded the Alpha Suffrage Club of Chicago, the first organization devoted to gaining the right to vote for African American women.

Queen Liliuokalani was the monarch of the territory of Hawaii when it was overthrown by a bloodless revolution.

1893 ▪ Queen Liliuokalani overthrown in bloodless revolution

Queen Liliuokalani was the monarch of the territory of Hawaii when it was overthrown by a bloodless revolution. Led by nine Americans, two Britons, and two Germans, the revolutionary effort was also aided by the U.S. Marines. Queen Liliuokalani was the last of the royal family of King Kamehameha to rule in Hawaii. (Kamehameha unified the local chiefs of Hawaii in 1795.) Liliuokalani was also known for writing a number of songs, including "Farewell to Thee" ("Aloha Oe"), which was popular in the United States in the 1950s.

1894 ▪ Sarah Grand coined phrase "new woman"

Sarah Grand (1854–1943) was born Frances Clarke to British parents in Donaghadee, Ireland. When she was 16 she married D. C. McFall, an army doctor. After 23 years of marriage she left her husband and became a writer. Using the pen name Sarah Grand, she wrote *The Heavenly Twins* (1893), which addressed the problem of syphilis (a sexually transmitted disease), and *The Beth Book* (1898), an autobiographical treatment of disillusionment with marriage. An advocate of women's emancipation (freedom), Grand has been credited with coining the phrase "new woman" in 1894 to describe a new generation of women like herself.

1896 ▪ Fannie Farmer published *The Boston Cooking-School Cook Book*

Fannie Merritt Farmer (1857–1915) was born in Boston, Massachusetts. Having suffered a stroke at the age of 16, Farmer was unable to attend college. She therefore stayed home and cooked. She later graduated from the Boston Cooking School, then returned as director of the school in 1891. While working there Farmer published *The Boston Cooking-School Cook Book* and introduced the concept of precise measurement. The cookbook assumed no previous knowledge of cooking on the part of its reader. The publisher, Little, Brown & Co., had little faith in Farmer's approach and required her to pay for the first printing of her book. In 1902 Farmer opened her own cooking school; to date millions of copies of her 700-page book have been sold.

1896 ▪ Producer-director Alice Guy screened film

Alice Guy (1873–1968), one of the world's first producer-directors of films, screened her movie *La Fée aux choux* ("The Cabbage Fairy"; released by the Gaumont film company) for the first time at the International Exhibition in Paris, France. Guy went on to make numerous one-reelers for Gaumont, even experimenting with sound as early as 1905. In 1910 she founded her own studio and production company, Solax, in Paris, and served as its first president and director-in-chief. The French government awarded her the Legion of Honor in 1953.

First Women's Bicycle Race

The first women's bicycle race started at Madison Square Garden in New York City on January 6, 1896. It drew the distaste of the League of American Wheelmen, a men's bicycle club. By the end of the race at midnight on January 12th, all 13 of the women starters had finished. The winner was Frankie Nelson, who rode over 418 miles.

1897 ▪ Hani Motoko, Japan's first woman newspaper reporter

Hani Motoko (1873–1957) was in the first graduating class of Japan's pioneer public high school for women, Tokyo Women's Normal School. After graduation she became a journalist. Initially hired as copy editor for the newspaper *Hochi shimbun,* she became Japan's first woman newspaper reporter when she was promoted in 1897. As a reporter she wrote about women, education, and religion. In 1901 she married her colleague at the newspaper, Hani Yoshikazu (1880–1955), who became her partner in journalistic and educational ventures. In 1903 Hani Motoko launched *Katei no tomo* ("Friend of the Household"), becoming its sole editor and writer. In 1921 the Hanis founded Jiyu Gakuen (Freedom Academy), an all-girls' boarding school. The purpose of the school was to cultivate "good wives and wise mothers," who could run a household without depending on servants.

1898 ▪ Lizzie Arlington signed baseball contract

Lizzie Arlington became the first woman to sign a contract in the professional minor leagues, where she played for several years. Women played baseball at the turn of the century in all-women's leagues.

1899 ▪ Lin Heier participated in Boxer Rebellion

Lin Heier was a member of the Red Lantern Society, a group of young female Chinese rebels who participated in the anti-Western Boxer Rebellion (1899–1901). The rebels were called "Boxers" because they believed that traditional martial arts techniques would protect them from Western bullets.

1899 ▪ Senda Berenson wrote rules for women's basketball

Senda Berenson (1868–1954) was born in Lithuania. After immigrating to the United States, she was a physical education teacher at Smith College. In 1893 she introduced her version of the game of basketball, modified for women, to her students. Basketball was originated by James Naismith in 1891. Berenson created the first official rules for girls in 1899 and then was appointed chair of the American Association of Education Committee on Basketball for Girls. She held the position for 12 years. Berenson wrote the first published rules for the sport, *Line Basket Ball for Women,* in 1901. For her contributions to women's basketball, she was inducted into the Naismith Hall of Fame and the Women's Sports Hall of Fame in 1984.

1899 ▪ Ida Kaminska, founder of Yiddish theaters, was born

Ida Kaminska (1899–?), an actor and benefactor in Yiddish theater, was born in Poland. (Yiddish is a language written in Hebrew characters and spoken by Jews of central and eastern European origin.) She founded the Warsaw Jewish Art Theater and the Ida Kaminska Theater, both in Warsaw, Poland. Forced to leave Europe because of anti-Semitism (discrimination against Jews), Kaminska moved to New York City, where she continued her work on behalf of Yiddish drama.

1900 ▪ Colette published first autobiographical novel

Sidonie Gabriel Colette (1873–1954), known simply as Colette, was a leading modernist (experimental) French author of the post-World War I era. In 1900 she published the first of her four autobiographical novels (1900–1904) about a girl named Claudine. Besides her autobiographical works, Colette wrote other famous novels, including *Cheri* (1920), *The Cat* (1933), and one of her best-known books, *Gigi* (1944). A film version of *Gigi* was made in 1958, starring Leslie Caron in the title role. After divorcing her first husband, Willy, in 1906, Colette became a music hall performer for eight years. She was the first woman president of the Goncourt Academy and the second woman to be named a grand officer of the French Foreign Legion.

Colette was the second woman to be named a grand officer of the French Foreign Legion.

1900 ▪ Tsuda Umeko founded Tsuda Women's University

Tsuda Umeko (1865–1929), a leader of women's education in Japan, founded Joshi Eigaku Juku (now Tsuda Women's University). Before founding the university in 1900, Umeko spent many years receiving an education and teaching in the United States and Japan. Tsuda Women's University made a significant contribution to women's higher education and the promotion of English-language instruction by preparing women as secondary school English teachers.

1901 ▪ Inuit artist Helen Kalvak was born

Helen Kalvak (1901–1984), the first Inuit (Eskimo) woman to chronicle the life of her people in art, was born in 1901. Kalvak began drawing when she was in her late sixties. She traveled throughout the Northwest Territories in Canada, creating over 3,000 pictures that convey the traditional culture and activities of the Copper Inuit. Kalvak's works stress her people's spiritual life, legends, and ceremonies. She was honored in 1975 with membership in the Royal Canadian Academy of Arts.

1901 ▪ Stella Franklin published *My Brilliant Career*

Stella Maria Miles Franklin (1879–1954) was born in Talbingo, New South Wales. Until the age of ten she lived on a farm with her family; then they moved to Sydney, Australia. Initially interested in nursing, she later turned to journalism and became involved in the feminist movement. In 1901 she wrote *My Brilliant Career,* a semiautobiographical novel about a teenage girl who rebels against the constraints of womanhood and marriage. Five years later Franklin moved to the United States. During World War I she worked in the Scottish Women's Hospital in Macedonia. In 1932 she returned permanently to Australia, where she again wrote novels under the pen name of "Brent of Bin Bin." *My Career Goes Bung,* the sequel to *My Brilliant Career,* appeared in 1946. *My Brilliant Career* was made into a film in 1979 and won several major awards.

1902 ▪ Helena Rubinstein opened first salon

Helena Rubinstein (1870–1965) was born into a Jewish family in Krakow, Poland. After studying medicine, she fled to rural Australia in 1894 to avoid an unwanted marriage. According to legend, she took along 12 pots of face cream made by her mother. Rubinstein's skin stayed so beautiful in the harsh Australian climate that people demanded the cream. In 1902 she opened a beauty salon in Melbourne, then expanded her business to London, England, in 1908 and Paris, France, in 1912. After World War I broke out in Europe, Rubinstein moved to New York City, where she began wholesale distribution of her products in 1917. By the end of World War II she had built cosmetics factories throughout the world and had accumulated a fortune of over 100 million dollars. In addition to running Helena Rubinstein Inc., Rubinstein established a foundation for support of the arts and education and endowed (gave money to) institutions for the poor.

1902 ▪ Florence Sabin appointed to faculty at Johns Hopkins University

Medical researcher Florence Rena Sabin (1871–1953) was born in Central City, Colorado. She graduated from Smith

College in 1893 and received her medical degree from Johns Hopkins University in Baltimore, Maryland, seven years later. In 1902 Sabin became the first female faculty member at Johns Hopkins, and in 1917 she was appointed the first female full professor at the university. From 1924 to 1926 Sabin served as the first female president of the American Association of Anatomists. She was also the first woman elected to the New York Academy of Sciences and the first female member of the Rockefeller Institute. After her retirement in 1938 Sabin devoted her efforts to enacting public health legislation in Colorado.

1903 ▪ Sara Josephine Baker founded public health agency

Sara Josephine Baker (1873–1945) was born in Poughkeepsie, New York, to a family of Quakers (members of a Christian sect that promotes justice, peace, and simplicity in living). In 1879, following the loss of her father and brother in a typhoid epidemic, she decided to become a doctor so she could support her mother and sister. After receiving her degree from New York Women's Medical College, she became the assistant health commissioner of New York in 1903. Baker worked on behalf of public health issues, helping to decrease the infant mortality rate on the East Side of New York City. One of her projects was establishing "milk stations," where nurses examined babies and distributed high-quality, low-cost milk. At first refused a lectureship at New York University (NYU) in 1915 because the institution did not admit women to its graduate program, Baker helped to change the university policy. She taught on the NYU faculty for 15 years. A recognized authority on child hygiene, she served on more than 25 children's health committees, including the League of Nations Health Committee (1922–1924). Baker was also the first woman to receive a doctorate in public health (1917).

Dr. Sara Josephine Baker helped to decrease the infant mortality rate on the East Side of New York City.

Marie Curie was the first person—male or female—to win two Nobel Prizes.

1903 ▪ Marie Curie won Nobel Prize

Marie Sklowdowska (1867–1934) was born into a poor family in Warsaw, Poland. After graduating from high school she worked for eight years as a governess and saved enough money to send her sister to school in Paris, France. Moving to Paris herself in 1891, Curie received a degree in physics from the Sorbonne two years later. A scholarship from Poland enabled her to continue her studies in mathematics. In 1894 she married Pierre Curie, with whom she discovered the radioactive properties of uranium.

Marie broke new ground when she conducted experiments with radiation for her doctoral thesis, isolating radioactive elements in minerals such as pitchblende and chalcocite. Pierre Curie quit his own work on piezoelectricity (electricity in crystalline substances such as quartz) to assist her. In 1898 the Curies announced the discovery of the new elements polonium (named for Marie's native country) and radium (an intensely radioactive mineral element). In 1903 they were awarded a Nobel Prize in physics for their discovery of radioactivity, an honor they shared with A. H. Becquerel, a colleague at the Sorbonne. Marie thus became the first woman to win a Nobel Prize in physics.

When her husband died in a streetcar accident in 1906, Marie Curie was appointed to fill his chair at the Sorbonne, making her the first woman in France to achieve this academic rank. Curie was also the first person—male or female—to win two Nobel Prizes: she was awarded the prize for chemistry in 1911 for the isolation of pure radium. Because the Curies had not taken precautions against exposure to radioactivity during their experiments, Marie began to experience symptoms of radiation sickness around 1898. She died of leukemia (a fatal disease of the white blood cells) in 1934.

1904 ▪ Evangeline Booth became Salvation Army commander

Evangeline Cora Booth (1865–1950) was born in Hackney, East London, England, the daughter of William Booth and Catherine Booth, founders of the Salvation Army. (The Salvation Army is an international religious and charitable group organized according to military procedures.) Rising through the ranks from the age of 15, Evangeline became the first woman to serve as commander of the Salvation Army in the United States. She held this post from 1904 until 1934, when she assumed worldwide leadership of the Salvation Army as international general. Retiring in 1939, Booth also wrote songs for the army and published several books.

1904 ▪ Ida Tarbell published *History of the Standard Oil Company*

Ida Minerva Tarbell (1857–1944) was born in Erie County, Pennsylvania. She studied at Allegheny College and the Sorbonne in Paris, then joined the staff of *McClure's Magazine* in 1894. Tarbell had previously published biographies of the French emperor Napoleon, French feminist Madame Roland, and U.S. president Abraham Lincoln. Her investigation of the tactics used by oil magnate John D. Rockefeller in building the Standard Oil Company was published in book form as *History of the Standard Oil Company* in 1904. Tarbell denounced Rockefeller's empire-building business tactics and contributed significantly to efforts to pass antitrust legislation (laws to prevent business monopolies) in the United States. In 1906 she joined other *McClure's* writers to found *American* magazine, in which she campaigned against big-business corruption. Her works on women's rights include *The Business of Being a Woman* (1912) and *The Ways of Women* (1915). Tarbell published her autobiography, *All in the Day's Work,* in 1939.

Ida Tarbell's writings contributed significantly to efforts to pass antitrust legislation.

1905 ▪ Tatiana Ehrenfest-Afanaseva wrote about theoretical physics

Tatiana Ehrenfest-Afanaseva (1876– 1964) was born in Kiev, Ukraine. Her father, a civil engineer, died when she was a child, and she went to live with a childless uncle who was a professor at the Polytechnical Institute in Saint Petersburg. Afanaseva attended the women's pedagogical (teaching) school and then the Women's Curriculum, where she excelled in mathematics. In 1902 she traveled to Germany for courses at the University of Göttingen, then renowned for mathematics and physics (the science of matter and energy). Two years later she married Paul Ehrenfest, a Jewish physics student.

In Saint Petersburg, Ehrenfest-Afanaseva raised two daughters and also took care of her mother and aunt. She published her first paper in theoretical physics in 1905, followed by other works in Russian and German. With her husband she authored a critique of statistical thermodynamics and helped illuminate how microscopic particles relate to the balance of matter. Although Ehrenfest-Afanaseva neither completed a doctorate nor held a regular university teaching position, her writings substantially enriched the field of theoretical physics.

1905 ▪ Renée Vivien published *A Woman Appeared to Me*

Renée Vivien (1877–1909) was born Pauline Mary Tarn in England in 1877. She studied in Paris, France, until her family moved to the United States. At age 21, Vivien returned to Paris and became involved with Natalie Barney, an American heiress. Barney and Vivien were part of the homosexual movement that emerged in the late nineteenth century. The two women dreamed of establishing a society of women poets dedicated to the ancient Greek poet Sappho and located on the island of Mytilene (Lesbos), where Sappho lived. Vivien learned Greek in order to read Sappho's work in the original language and eventually translated the ancient poetry into French. (*Also see entry dated c. 610 B.C.: Sappho wrote poetry.*)

1905 ▪ **Elizabeth Gurley Flynn helped found IWW**

Elizabeth Gurley Flynn (1890–1964) was born in Concord, New Hampshire, into a family of socialists. (Socialism is a political doctrine that champions the removal of private property in a quest to attain a classless society.) In 1905 she became a founding member of the Industrial Workers of the World (IWW), whose members were often referred to as "Wobblies." Three years later Flynn married John Archibald Jones, but they were eventually divorced. She participated in several historic labor actions over the years, including the 1909 strike of New York City waistmakers; the 1912 strikes of Lowell and Lawrence textile mill workers; the 1913 strike of the Paterson, New Jersey, silk workers; the 1916 Mesabi Range miners' strike; and the 1926 Passaic, New Jersey, textile workers' strike. In 1952 Flynn was tried and convicted under the Smith Act in New York City and then spent 30 months in a West Virginia federal women's prison.

1905 ▪ **Tennis star Helen Wills Moody was born**

Helen Wills (1905–) was born in Centerville, California. A truly great tennis player, she had a record of eight Wimbledon singles titles, seven U.S. women's singles titles, four French championships, and a gold medal at the 1924 Olympics. She added "Moody," her husband's surname, to her own name during her marriage from 1929 to 1937. Challenging clothing requirements for women tennis players, she set the standard for less restricting attire on the courts. She is also credited with bringing women's tennis to an international level of exposure and acceptance.

1906 ▪ **Mother Ella Bloor began reform efforts**

Ella Reeve Bloor (1862–1951) was born on Staten Island, New York. She married at age 19 and later had four children. In 1906 she worked with Richard Bloor in Chicago stockyards (a yard in which cattle, sheep, pigs, or horses are kept until they can be slaughtered, butchered, and shipped to market) to gather evidence used by writer Upton Sinclair in *The Jungle* (1906). Sinclair's book provided a shocking account of conditions in the meat-packing industry.

In 1906 Ella Bloor worked to gather evidence used by writer Upton Sinclair for his book The Jungle.

In 1909 Bloor joined the Women's Suffrage Association and became chair of the Department of Working Women. During World War I she joined Elizabeth Gurley Flynn and other pacifists to founded the Workers Defense Union. Nicknamed "Mother" Bloor, she published several books of her own, including her autobiography, *We Are Many* (1940).

1906 ▪ Madame C. J. Walker began selling hair care products

Sarah Breedlove (1867–1919; later known as Madame C. J. Walker) was born in Delta, Louisiana. The daughter of former slaves who died when she was seven, she married a man named McWilliams at the age of fourteen. In 1885 she gave birth to a daughter, Lelia. Two years later, after the death of her husband, Walker moved to St. Louis, Missouri, where she worked as a washerwoman. Like many black women of the era, Walker straightened her hair by twisting it and wrapping it with string. This procedure caused hair loss, however, so she developed her own hair-straightening product known as "Wonderful Hair Grower."

Eventually quitting her job as a laundress, she devoted her energies to making other hair care products for black hair. In 1906 she married Charles Joseph Walker, a journalist in Denver, Colorado, who helped her build a huge mail-order business. She also adopted a new professional name for herself and her enterprise—Madame C. J. Walker. In 1908 Walker opened an office in Pittsburgh, Pennsylvania, and two years later established laboratories in Indianapolis, Indiana. She is remembered as the first black woman to become a millionaire.

1907 ▪ Qiu Jin was assassinated by Chinese government

Qiu Jin (1875–1907) was born in China and studied in Japan. While in Japan she edited a journal and engaged in var-

ious political activities. After returning home she spoke out against the men of China who had failed to protect the nation during years of political and social turmoil; women, she concluded, could no longer rely upon men. While participating in an unsuccessful uprising, she was killed by government troops. Qiu Jin was perhaps the most famous woman radical in China.

Olympic Committee Recognized Female Athletes

In 1908 the International Olympic Committee gave official recognition to women athletes. American women, however, were not recognized until 1920, partly because the U.S. Amateur Athletic Union (AAU) did not sanction women's swimming until 1914. At earlier Olympics Games, a few women participated "unofficially" in events such as running, tennis, golf, yachting, and archery. After the Interim Games in 1906, women were officially allowed to compete.

1907 ▪ Annette Kellerman favored bare swimwear

Annette Marie Sarah Kellerman (1886–1975) was born in Sydney, Australia. In 1905 she held world records in all women's swimming events. Two years later she was arrested on a Boston, Massachusetts, beach for wearing a brief, one-piece swimsuit. The subsequent publicity helped change the laws that encased women in neck-to-knee swimwear. Kellerman regarded this as her greatest achievement.

1908 ▪ Annie Smith Peck set climbing records

Annie Smith Peck (1850–1935) was born in Providence, Rhode Island. Educated in Athens, Greece, she taught Greek at Purdue University and Smith College. At the age of forty-five she began climbing in the Alps and, in 1902, co-founded the Alpine Club. Six years later she was the first person to climb the north peak of Mount Huascaran in Peru, an altitude of 21,812 feet. At the time, this was the highest altitude reached by any climber in the Western Hemisphere.

1909 ▪ Selma Lagerlöf won Nobel Prize

Selma Lagerlöf (1858–1940) was born in Märback, Sweden. Because she was disabled, she led a sheltered childhood. After working as a teacher for ten years, she published the novel *Gösta Berlings saga* ("The Story of Gösta Berling") in 1891. Lagerlöf's later books include *The Rings of the Lowenskolds* (1931) and a classic children's book, *Nils Holgerssons underbara genom Sverige* (1907; "The Wonderful Adventures of Nils"). Honored for her sagas and legendary narratives, in 1909 she became the first woman to win the Nobel Prize for literature. She used her prize money to buy back her family home, which her father had been forced to sell. Lagerlöf was also the first woman member of the Swedish Academy (1914).

In 1908 Annie Peck Smith was the first person to climb the north peak of Mount Huascaran in Peru, an altitude of 21,812 feet.

1910 ▪ Poet Marina Tsvetaeva published first collection

Marina Tsvetaeva (1892–1941) grew up in Moscow, Russia, where her father was a professor and her mother was a pianist. Tsvetaeva traveled throughout Europe with her family and entered the Sorbonne in Paris, France, at the age of sixteen. When she was 25, she married Sergei Efron, an army officer who took part in the resistance to the Bolshevik regime in the

Russian Revolution of 1917. (The Bolsheviks were Russian revolutionaries who led the Russian Revolution of 1917, which resulted in the formation of the communist Soviet state. Communism is a system of government in which the state controls the means of production and the distribution of goods. It clashes with the American ideal of capitalism, which is based on private ownership and a free market system.)

Fleeing from the new Soviet Union in 1922, Tsvetaeva and her husband settled first in Prague, Czechoslovakia, and then in Paris, where they lived in poverty. While abroad, she began publishing the poetry that established her as one of the finest Russian poets of the twentieth century. Tsvetaeva's poems are famous for their rhythm, originality, and directness.

1910 ▪ Charlotte Vetter Gulick cofounded Campfire Girls

Charlotte Vetter Gulick (1866–1928) and her husband, Luther Halsey Gulick, founded the Camp Fire Girls in Maine. It was the first nonsectarian (nonreligious) organization for girls in the United States. Camp Fire Girls stress character development and good mental and physical health.

1910 ▪ Anna Jarvis initiated Mother's Day

In 1907 West Virginian Anna Jarvis held a memorial service for her mother in Grafton, West Virginia. The service took place on the second Sunday in May, two years after her mother died. Jarvis later launched a successful letter-writing campaign to urge legislators to create a formal holiday to honor mothers. By 1911 nearly all the states joined West Virginia in celebrating Mother's Day. In 1915 President Woodrow Wilson signed the law making Mother's Day a national holiday.

1910 ▪ Yoshioka Yayoi established medical school in Japan

Physician, educator, and public official Yoshioka Yayoi (1871–1959) founded Japan's first medical school for women,

Tokyo Joigakko (later called Tokyo Joshi Igaku Semmon Gakko). During her 50-year tenure as president, her school educated more than 7,000 women doctors. Since Yayoi believed in the "do and learn" principle, her students were even present to learn from her own experiences of childbirth and miscarriage. Much public criticism was leveled against women who engaged in "grossly unladylike" activities like dissecting cadavers, and Yayoi countered these criticisms through the school newspaper, *Joikai*. In 1955 Yayoi received the Fujin Bunka Sho (Women's Cultural Award), Japan's highest honor for women.

1910 ▪ Emmeline Freda du Faur climbed Mount Cook

Australian mountaineer Emmeline Freda du Faur (1882–1935) was born and educated in Sydney, Australia, where she spent most of her life devoted to rock climbing. In 1906, during a visit to New Zealand, du Faur decided to climb Mount Cook. At the time her decision was considered scandalous not only because her mountain guide was a man but also because it was understood that mountaineers wore trousers. These difficulties were overcome when du Faur hired a porter (equipment carrier) to act as chaperone and agreed to undertake all her expeditions wearing a skirt. On December 3, 1910, she climbed Mount Cook in the record time of six hours.

1911 ▪ Leonora O'Reilly responded to tragedy

On March 25, 1911, fire broke out on the eighth floor of the Triangle Shirtwaist Company in New York City, causing one of the worst industrial accidents of the time. Of the 500 workers crowded into the top three floors, 146 of them died.

Expanding the Vote to Women in the United States

During the early twentieth century 14 U.S. states gave women the right to vote. These states were:

1910 Washington

1911 California

1912 Oregon

1912 Kansas

1912 Arizona

1913 Alaska

1914 Nevada

1914 Montana

1917 New York

1917 Arkansas

1918 Michigan

1918 South Dakota

1918 Oklahoma

1918 Texas

Full voting rights were not granted to women nationwide until 1920.

Of over 500 workers, 146 women and children died when fire broke out at the Triangle Shirtwaist Company on March 25, 1911.

Most were women and children. Their deaths resulted from unsafe building conditions that included faulty doors and blocked or rickety fire escapes. A year earlier workers at the Triangle Company were engaged in the "Uprising of the 20,000." Two of their demands addressed the problems with the doors and fire escapes. Unfortunately, however, the strike was unsuccessful, and the Triangle Company refused to listen to the workers' demands.

This appalling disaster prompted many women to join the struggle for improved factory working conditions. Among these women was Leonora O'Reilly, a lifelong union activist who was instrumental in passing the first factory inspection law.

1911 ▪ Elizabeth Glendower Evans campaigned for minimum wage

Elizabeth Glendower Evans (1856–1937) was an American reformer, suffragist (fighter for women's right to vote), and labor organizer. She married in 1882 but was widowed just four years later. Evans was appointed to the Massachusetts reformatory system board of trustees. In 1911 she worked with Florence Kelley in a campaign in Massachusetts that resulted in the first minimum wage law for women passed in the United States.

An active member of the Women's Trade Union League, Evans participated in many strikes. These included the 1910 weavers' strike in Roxbury, Massachusetts, and the 1912 textile (clothmaking) workers' strike in Lawrence, Massachusetts. For over 25 years she was a contributing editor to *La Follette's Weekly Magazine,* a reformist labor publication put out by Senator Robert La Follette and Belle La Follette. She also lobbied on behalf of the American Woman Suffrage Association and was a national director of the American Civil Liberties Union.

1912 ▪ Anna Akhmatova published poems

Anna Andreyevna Gorenko (1889–1966), who later wrote under the pseudonym Anna Akhmatova, was born in Odessa, Russia. After studying in Kiev and then moving to St. Petersburg, she married writer Nicholas Gumilev. Together they started the Acmeist movement. Akhmatova published numerous poems between 1912 and 1923, including "Vecher" (title means "Evening"), "Chokti" (title means "The Rosary"), and "Belaya Staya" (title means "The White Flock"). She was famous for her clarity of expression and honest portrayal of intense human emotions.

In 1917, at the height of Akhmatova's writing career, the Communist Revolution began in Russia. (The Communist Revolution was a political movement that resulted in the overthrowing of the aristocracy and formation of the Union of Soviet Socialist Republics [USSR] under a communist government. Communism is a system of government in which the state controls the means of production and the distribution of goods. It clashes with the American ideal of capitalism, which is based on private ownership and a free market system.) During this time Akhmatova's marriage ended and her former husband was executed for counter-revolutionary activities.

Official Soviet critics denounced her poetry, which was only rarely published in Russia after 1923. Following the death of Soviet dictator Joseph Stalin in 1954, Akhmatova and her work gradually regained respect and popularity in the Soviet Union. By the time of her death in 1966, Akhmatova was widely hailed as the greatest woman poet in Russian literature.

1912 ▪ Maria Montessori wrote *The Montessori Method*

Maria Montessori (1870–1952) was born in Ancona, Italy. In 1896 Montessori became the first woman in Italy to receive a medical degree, after which she began her work in children's education. By 1906 she had opened her first *Casa dei Bambinin* ("children's house") in a run-down area of Rome. Six years later Montessori published her ideas about education in *Il metodo della pedagogia scientifica* ("The Montessori Method"). Her emphasis rested on a child's own natural motivation and creative potential. In the classroom Montessori gave children wood cylinders to promote small-muscle development, beads to increase counting skills, and blocks arranged to strengthen eye movement for reading. Initially teaching only young children, Montessori developed a system for the instruction of older pupils as well. Her methods were eventually adopted in Montessori schools throughout the world. After retiring in 1934 Montessori moved to the Netherlands.

1912 ▪ Emmeline Pankhurst arrested for political activities

Emmeline Goulden (1857–1928) was born in Manchester, England. In 1879 she married Richard Marsden Pankhurst, a judge and the author of the first women's suffrage (voting rights) bill in Great Britain. Emmeline began her feminist activities in 1889, when she founded the Women's Franchise League. In 1903 she and her daughter Christine started the Women's Social and Political Union (WSPU). (Another daughter, Sylvia, also became a prominent suffragist.) At first the WSPU was a peaceful organization. However, by 1909 Pankhurst and her allies were condoning militant (supporting warlike) measures to acquire women's suffrage.

In 1912 Pankhurst was imprisoned for her activities, and she began a hunger strike. After her release she began to campaign for women's suffrage again. In 1916 Parliament finally permitted women over the age of 30 to vote. The age minimum was lowered to 21 in 1928, the year of Pankhurst's death, when the People Act granted voting equality to women. Pankhurst published her autobiography, *My Own Story,* in 1914.

1912 ▪ Juliette Low organized first Girl Scout troop

Juliette (Magille Kinzie) Gordon (1860–1927) was born in Savannah, Georgia. In 1886 she married William M. Low, but they were unhappy together and she spent most of her time traveling. Throughout her life she was troubled with deafness because of an early mistreatment of an ear infection. In 1911 Low met Robert Baden-Powell, the British general who had founded the Boy Scouts three years earlier. Envisioning a similar organization for girls, Low organized the first American group of Girl Scouts in Savannah in 1912. Her niece, Daisy

(Margaret) Gordon, became the first American Girl Scout when she joined the organization. Low was president of the Girl Scouts of America until her death in 1927.

1913 ▪ Marguerite Davis codiscovered vitamins A and B

Marguerite Davis (1887–1967) was born in Racine, Wisconsin. She received a bachelor of science degree from the University of California at Berkeley in 1910, then enrolled at the University of Wisconsin for graduate studies. During her time at Wisconsin she began her work with Elmer Verner McCollum, who had been studying nutrition for several years. In 1913 Davis and McCollum discovered a factor in some fats that apparently was essential to life. Because the substance differed chemically from one described earlier by other scientists, they named theirs A and the other B. These were later called vitamins A and B—A being fat soluble (meaning it would dissolve in fat) and B being water soluble (meaning it would dissolve in water). The identification of A and B led later to the discovery of the other vitamins and their specific roles in nutrition, as well as which foods contain them.

1913 ▪ Henrietta Leavitt developed star classification standard

Henrietta Swan Leavitt (1868–1921) was born in Lancaster, Massachusetts. Her father was a minister, and she was educated at Radcliffe College, where she became interested in astronomy (the study of the solar system). Starting as a volunteer at the Harvard Observatory, she joined the observatory staff in 1902, then advanced to head of the department of photometry (measurement of the intensity of light).

Leavitt developed a system that measured the relationship between the brightness of Cepheid variable stars (a class of pulsating stars with periods of brightness that last from a few days to several months) and the length of their period of pulsation (alternate increase and decrease of light). In 1912 she reported a direct relationship between the brightness of a star and the length of its pulsation. The International Committee on Photographic Magnitudes then voted to adopt Leavitt's system for their Astrographic Map of the Sky. They used it to measure the distance between Earth and the stars and to determine the size of the Milky Way (the combined light of the billions of stars in our galaxy).

1913 ▪ Amy Lowell wrote Imagist verse

Amy Lowell (1874–1925) was born in Brookline, Massachusetts. Her family was wealthy and influential—her brother Abbott became a respected political scientist, and another brother, Percival, was a prominent astronomer. Lowell traveled extensively throughout Europe with her parents. By the early 1900s she had gained interest in the Imagist poetry movement, in which poetic expression was rendered through clear, precise images. She corresponded with prominent Imagist poets H. D. (Hilda Doolittle), Richard Aldington, and Ezra Pound, who were writing in England. Lowell herself began to write poems with a technique she called "unrhymed cadence" (also known as free verse). Among her published collections are *A Dome of Many-Colored Glass* (1912) and *Sword Blades and Poppy Seeds* (1914). In addition, Lowell wrote several prose works, among them *The French Poets* (1915), *Tendencies in Modern Poetry* (1917), and a biography of British poet John Keats (1925). *What's O'Clock* (1925) was awarded the Pulitzer Prize after the author's death in 1925. Lowell also held the distinction of being the first woman to lecture on modernist verse in the United States.

Amy Lowell was the first woman to lecture on modernist verse in the United States.

1913 ▪ Anna Pavlova introduced Western dance in the East

Anna Pavlova (1882–1931) was born in St. Petersburg, Russia, where she studied dance at the Imperial Ballet School. In 1899 she joined the Imperial Ballet and became the prima ballerina (lead dancer) by 1906. Within a year she was interna-

tionally famous for roles in such works as *The Dying Swan* by choreographer (dance composer) Michel Fokine. In 1909 Pavlova joined the Ballet Russe, which was headed by famed choreographer Sergei Diaghilev. She then formed her own company, touring the world and introducing Western dance to countries such as Egypt, Japan, China, and India. Pavlov's tours included performances in outlying areas as well as in capital cities in order to encourage a broad appreciation of classical ballet. Her style of dance, which involved graceful, poetic movement, strongly influenced the image of the ballerina.

1913 ▪ Helen Keller helped the blind and deaf

Helen Keller (1880–1968) was born in Tuscumbia, Alabama. She became blind and deaf as the result of a high fever when she was nineteen months old. With the assistance of Anne Sullivan Macy, a teacher of the blind who came to live with the Keller family in 1887, Keller learned to communicate.

Her progress was slow at first, but she eventually mastered the alphabet through hand signals from Sullivan. Keller also was able to speak by feeling, then imitating, other people's tongue and lip movements. In 1903 she published her autobiography, *The Story of My Life.* After graduating with high honors from Radcliffe College in 1904, Keller continued writing about blindness. During a campaign to raise funds for the American Foundation for the Blind in 1913, Keller began her career as a respected lecturer and scholar. With Sullivan almost constantly at her side, Keller devoted the remainder of her long life to working for the blind and deaf. The story of Keller and Sullivan has been told on stage and screen as *The Miracle Worker.*

1915 ▪ Lillian Gish appeared in feature film

Lillian Gish (1896–1993) was born in Springfield, Ohio. She began her stage career at age six and in 1912 became a silent film actress. Three years later Gish appeared in the first modern motion picture, *Birth of a Nation,* by pioneering filmmaker D. W. Griffith. In most of her films Gish played a young maiden in peril, and she became famous for her long blonde hair and angelic face. Between 1919 and 1921 she appeared in all but two of Griffith's films, including *Broken Blossoms* (1919), *Way Down East* (1920), and *Orphans of the Storm* (1921). Gish received a special Oscar in 1970 for her lifetime work in film. In 1987 she starred in her one hundred and fourth film, *The Whales of August,* with legendary actress Bette Davis. Gish was 91 at the time.

In 1915 Lillian Gish appeared in the first modern motion picture, Birth of a Nation, *directed by D. W. Griffith.*

1916 ▪ Dorothy Parker joined *Vogue* magazine

Dorothy Parker (1893–1967) was born in West End, New Jersey. Although she did not attend school after the age of fourteen, she gained wide knowledge of literature by reading on her own. She also wrote poetry, and in 1916, after selling some poems to *Vogue* magazine, she was given a job writing photo captions at the New York City office. The following year Parker became the drama critic for *Vanity Fair* magazine, where she met literary figures Robert Benchley and Robert Sherwood. The trio formed the famous "Round Table" group, which met daily for lunch at the Algonquin Hotel in New York City. Parker continued to publish poetry as well as short stories and screenplays, and she became known for her wit and sarcasm. Twice married, Parker led a troubled life. Upon her death she left her considerable estate to civil rights leader Martin Luther King, Jr.(1929–1968).

1916 ▪ Activist Emily Murphy appointed magistrate

Emily Gowan Murphy (1868–1933) was born in Cookstown, Ontario, Canada, into a prominent legal family. In 1887 she married Arthur Murphy, and they moved to Alberta in 1907. Emily Murphy became a frequent contributor of book reviews and articles to a variety of Canadian magazines and newspapers. She later adopted the pen name "Janey Canuck" and published four popular books of personal accounts. Throughout her life Murphy was able to combine her family life, her passion for writing, and various reform activities. She was involved in the establishment and growth of many professional and volunteer women's organizations.

A self-taught legal expert, Murphy became the first woman police magistrate (administrator of laws) for Edmonton, then for Alberta, and finally in 1916 for the entire British empire. She was an opponent of narcotics, prostitution, and organized crime. A lawyer once challenged her authority, telling her that because she was a woman she was not recognized as "a person" under the laws of the British empire. "Judge Murphy" then embarked on a decade-long quest to have women declared legal persons and therefore made eligible for appointed positions.

1917 ▪ Tsarina Alexandra triggered Russian Revolution

Alix, princess of Hesse-Darmstadt (1872–1918) was born in Germany. In 1894 she married Tsar (emperor) Nicholas

II of Russia and took the name Alexandra. The tsarina (empress) gave birth to four daughters and a son, Alexis. Alexis suffered from hemophilia (a hereditary defect that delays blood clotting). In her search for a cure, Alexandra came under the influence of a "holy man" named Rasputin, who claimed he could control Alexis's bleeding. Alexandra's dependence on Rasputin (1871?–1916) became a public scandal. While Nicholas was at the front during World War I (1914–1918), Alexandra took control of the Russian government. Her dismissal of competent ministers and the appointment of Rasputin's henchmen led to the collapse of the tsarist regime. In 1917 the tsar was overthrown by a provisional (temporary) government. After the Bolsheviks (a radical group committed to violent overthrow of the government) took over Russia later that year, Nicholas, Alexandra, and their children were imprisoned. The entire family was executed in 1918.

1917 ▪ Loretta Walsh enlisted in U.S. Navy

Loretta Walsh (born in 1898), the first woman to enlist in the U.S. Navy, served in the military during World War I (1914–1918). For a few months after the United States entered the war, the navy was short-staffed and therefore permitted women to enlist, but they could only serve on U.S. soil. Walsh was a yeoman (one who performs clerical tasks) in charge of recruiting for the Naval Coastal Defense Reserve.

1917 ▪ Jeannette Rankin elected to U.S. House of Representatives

Jeannette Rankin (1880–1973) was born near Missoula, Montana. After being educated at the New York School of Philanthropy, Rankin worked as a social worker in Seattle, Washington. A noted suffragist (one who supported women's right to vote) and pacifist (antiwar activist), she first became active in women's issues in the early 1900s. In 1916 she took office as the first female member of the U.S. Congress. She served as a congresswoman-at-large from 1917 to 1919, leaving after one term. Rankin was reelected to the U.S. House of

Representatives in 1940, also for one term. During her service she voted against American participation in World War I (1914–1918). She was also the only member of Congress to vote against entering World War II in 1942. And in the midst of the Vietnam War she led the 1968 Jeanette Rankin March in Washington, D.C., during which 5,000 women protested U.S. involvement in Vietnam's civil war.

1919 ▪ Mary Pickford cofounded United Artists

American actress Mary Pickford (1893–1979) was born Gladys Mary Smith in Toronto, Ontario. Known as "America's Sweetheart," Pickford appeared in such silent films as *Tess of the Storm Country* (1922) and *Little Annie Rooney* (1925). In 1919, along with her husband, actor Douglas Fairbanks, and famous film comedian Charlie Chaplin, Pickford formed the United Artists (UA) film studio. She became UA's star, studio owner, executive producer, and director. In the prime of life, though, Pickford retreated from her film career. She was the first performer ever to become a millionaire from acting. Her autobiographical writings include *My Rendezvous with Life* (1935) and *Sunshine and Shadow* (1955).

1919 ▪ Delilah Leontium Beasley wrote history of African Americans

Self-taught historian Delilah Leontium Beasley (1867–1934) wrote the first history of African Americans in California, *The Negro Trail-Blazers of California*. In her book Beasley reminds readers that seven of the twenty-nine soldiers of the De Anza expedition to California in 1775 were of African descent and that African Americans played a major role in the history of California.

1920 ▪ Georgia O'Keeffe created controversial paintings

Georgia O'Keeffe (1887–1986) was born in Sun Prairie, Wisconsin. After studying painting at several art schools, she took up painting full time in 1918. She married photographer and art dealer Alfred Stieglitz four years later. O'Keeffe gained notice for her large, erotic flower canvases. (Eroticism is the arousal of sexual desire. O'Keeffe's paintings are often said to resemble naked human forms and are frequently associated with human sexuality.) She also became known for her symbolic still lifes—many of them featuring desert flowers and animal bones—set in the American West, where she began painting in the 1940s. Among her most famous works are *Black Iris* and *Summer Days*. In addition O'Keeffe was the subject of over 500 photographs taken by Stieglitz.

Georgia O'Keeffe became known for her symbolic still lifes, many of which feature desert flowers and animal bones.

1921 ▪ Edith Wharton won Pulitzer Prize

Edith Newbold Jones (c. 1861–1937) was born into a wealthy family in New York City. After being educated at home and in Europe, she married Edward Wharton in 1885. They traveled extensively, settling in Paris in 1907. Six years later they were divorced. Wharton formed a close friendship with great American novelist Henry James, who supported her own interest in becoming a writer. Wharton published her first work, a collection of short stories titled *The Greater Inclination,* in 1899. She then turned to writing novels and achieved popular success and critical recognition for her book about New York society, *The House of Mirth* (1905). Wharton went on to write 50 books during her career, among them *Ethan Frome* (1911) and *The Age of Innocence* (1920), which won the Pulitzer Prize for literature in 1921. Her autobiography, *A Backwards Glance,* was published in 1934. Wharton is now considered one of the most important twentieth-century American novelists. Film versions of her novels include *Ethan Frome* (1992), with Liam Neeson in the title role, and *The Age of Innocence* (1993), starring Daniel Day-Lewis and Winona Ryder.

1924 ▪ Alexandra David-Neel entered Lhasa, Tibet

Alexandra David-Neel (1869–1968) was born in Paris, France. After studying Sanskrit (an ancient Indian language) in

In 1924 Alexandra David-Neel successfully crossed into Tibet disguised as an old woman.

Sri Lanka and India, she toured internationally as an opera singer. In 1904 she married Phillipe François Neel, who sponsored her travels in Europe. David-Neel returned to India in 1911 to study Tibetan Buddhism (an ancient Asian religion founded in India) with the Dalai Lama (the spiritual head of Buddhism). Because she had entered Tibet illegally (Westerners were forbidden to travel in that country), she was expelled from India in 1916. With her lifelong servant Yongden, a Sikkimese student lama (Buddhist monk), she traveled in Burma, Japan, Korea, and China. In 1924 she successfully crossed into Tibet, entering the holy city of Lhasa disguised as an old Tibetan woman. She finally sent a letter to her husband, who had not heard from her in two years. The first European woman to enter Lhasa, David-Neel went on to write several books about her experiences, including *My Journey to Lhasa* (1927).

1924 ▪ Ichikawa Fusae organized Women's Suffrage League

Ichikawa Fusae (1893–1981) was a feminist, suffragist (supporter of women's right to vote), and politician born in Japan. She organized the Fusen Kakutoku Domei (Women's Suffrage League) in 1924. As leader of this organization, she worked for the next 16 years to persuade legislators to extend women's political rights. After World War II (1939–1945) she was a participant in the discussions that resulted in the 1947 constitution that granted women the vote and equal rights in Japan.

1925 ▪ Coco Chanel created "little black dress"

Coco Chanel (1883–1971) was born Gabrielle Chanel in France. She was orphaned as a young child, and worked with her sister as a milliner (hat maker) until 1912. After briefly operating her own hat shop in Paris, France, Chanel opened a couture house (dress-designing shop) in Deauville, France, in

1913. She served as a nurse during World War I (1914–1918), then started another couture house in Paris in 1924. Within a year Chanel had revolutionized fashion with clothing for the "new modern woman"—simple, comfortable garments that did not require corsets. Among her creations was the understated and elegant "little black dress," which Chanel introduced in 1926. The dress was an immediate success because women could wear it for a variety of occasions.

c. 1928 ▪ Biochemist Wanda Farr solved scientific mystery

Wanda Farr (b. 1895) was born in New Matamoras, Ohio. Farr had initially decided to attend medical school, but her family insisted she not become a doctor, fearing she would be exposed to tuberculosis. Instead she earned a degree in botany (the science of plant life) from Ohio University in 1915 and a master's degree, also in botany, from Columbia University three years later. Following her husband's death in 1928 Farr worked with the U.S. Department of Agriculture as a cotton technologist at the Boyce Thompson Institute, which was then located in Yonkers, New York. While working at the institute she solved a major scientific mystery in botany by showing that the substance cellulose, an important compound found in all plants, is made by tiny, cellular structures called plastids. In 1956 she founded her own laboratory, the Farr Cytochemistry Lab in Nyack, New York.

1928 ▪ Elsa Schiaparelli unveiled her first creation

Elsa Schiaparelli (1890–1973) was born in Rome, Italy. Schiaparelli's gifts as a writer, sculptor, and painter emerged early, but she was inclined instead to "invent dresses or costumes." In 1928 she produced her first fashion creation, a black, short-sleeved sweater knitted with the pattern of a but-

By 1925 Chanel had revolutionized fashion with clothing for the "new modern woman."

In the 1920s Margaret Mead undertook expeditions to study tribal people in New Guinea and Samoa.

terfly bow around the neckline. The success of these sweaters prompted Schiaparelli to experiment further with fashion designs. She became famous for integrating elements of contemporary art with bold colors, inventive accessories, and surprisingly simple lines to create her popular fashions.

1928 ▪ Margaret Mead published *Coming of Age in Samoa*

Margaret Mead was born in Philadelphia, Pennsylvania. She worked as a curator of ethnology (the study of ethnic groups) at the American Museum of Natural History in New York City from 1926 to 1964. In the 1920s she undertook expeditions to study tribal people in New Guinea and Samoa. Mead wrote about her work in *Coming of Age in Samoa* (1928) and *Growing Up in New Guinea* (1930). Her books triggered much public debate because she argued that the human personality is determined by cultural conditioning rather than heredity. Mead was well known for her ability to make scientific fact understandable to a lay audience. In recent years, however, questions have been raised about the validity of her early research.

1929 ▪ Eleanor Roosevelt became "ambassadress"

Anna Eleanor Roosevelt (1884–1962) was born in New York City to a wealthy and prominent family. In 1905 she married Franklin Delano Roosevelt (FDR), with whom she had six children. In 1929 FDR was elected governor of New York. Because he had lost the use of his legs during a bout with polio (a virus that affects the spinal cord and, in turn, interferes with muscle movement) in 1921, he sent Eleanor on countless official inspection trips to act as his "ambassadress." Her personal reports from the field during the height of the Great Depression (a period of severe economic slowdown in the United States that lasted from 1929 to the early 1940s) helped shape the state's social policies.

In 1932 FDR was elected to his first of four consecutive terms as U.S. president. As first lady, Eleanor Roosevelt took full advantage of her position to champion the rights of women and minorities and to work for international cooperation. After her husband's death in 1945, she became active in the United Nations (a world peace organization designed to promote global cooperation and security), serving in various positions, including U.S. representative to the General Assembly (1946–1952). In addition to writing a newspaper column that appeared in 140 papers throughout the United States, Roosevelt also published numerous books, among them her autobiography, *On My Own* (1962).

1930 ▪ Dorothy Eustis introduced seeing eye dogs

Dorothy Harrison Eustis (c. 1886–1946) became interested in guide dogs for the blind in 1927, when she visited a school in Potsdam, Germany, that was training dogs to help the disabled. After writing an article about guide dogs for the *Saturday Evening Post,* Eustis arranged to train a dog for a blind insurance salesman living in the United States. She briefly ran a school to train guide dogs in Nashville, Tennessee, before moving the school to Morristown, New Jersey.

1931 ▪ Verne "Jackie" Mitchell played major league baseball

On April 1, 1931, pitcher Verne "Jackie" Mitchell signed a contract to pitch for Tennessee's Memphis Lookouts (a team in baseball's Southern Association), thus becoming the first woman to play major league baseball. In an exhibition game against the New York Yankees, she struck out Babe Ruth and Lou Gehrig, who were both legendary hitters.

Canadian Women Were Declared "Persons"

On October 18, 1929, the Judicial Committee of the Privy Council (JCPC) in England—the highest court of appeal on questions related to Canadian law at the time—reversed a 1928 decision of the Canadian Supreme Court and declared women to be "persons" under the 1867 British North America Act (the basis for Canada's constitution). This cleared the way for women to be appointed to the Canadian Senate, a non-elected body similar to Britain's House of Lords. Cairine Wilson was appointed the first woman senator in 1930.

1932 ▪ "Babe" Didrikson-Zaharias won two gold medals

Mildred Ella Didrikson (1914–1956), nicknamed "Babe," was born in Port Arthur, Texas. As a result of her success in the 1931 American Athletic Union (AAU) championships, she was placed on the U.S. track and field team for the 1932 Summer Olympic Games in Los Angeles, California. In the three events she entered she won two gold medals—one for the javelin throw and the other for 80-meter hurdles—as well as a silver medal. In 1935 Didrikson took up golf, winning 17 golf tournaments between 1946 and 1948. She turned professional in 1948 and the following year cofounded the Ladies Professional Golf Association (LPGA). Didrikson married George Zaharias in 1938.

In 1952 Didrikson-Zaharias was diagnosed with rectal cancer. Despite being in great pain, she played in—and took top honors at—five golf competitions. By 1954, however, the cancer had spread to her spine. She died at age 42.

In 1943 Jacqueline
Cochran was the first
woman to pilot a bomber
across the Atlantic Ocean.

1932 ▪ Jacqueline Cochran earned pilot's license

Jacqueline Cochran (1910–1980) was born in Pensacola, Florida. She worked as a beautician and in her spare time qualified for her pilot's license, which she obtained in 1932. After starting her own cosmetics company in 1934, Cochran achieved many firsts as a pioneering aviator. In 1935 she was the first woman to fly in the Bendix transcontinental air race across the United States. In 1943 she was the first woman to pilot a bomber across the Atlantic Ocean from the United States to England. And in 1953 she broke the sound barrier when she flew an F-86 Saber jet at 760 miles per hour over the Rogers Dry Lake near Edwards Air Force Base in California.

1932 ▪ Amelia Earhart flew across Atlantic Ocean

Amelia Earhart (1898–1937) was born in Atchison, Kansas. After working first as a nurse and then as a social worker, she embarked on a career as an aviator. On May 22,

1932, she achieved her greatest victory when she became the first woman to fly an airplane across the Atlantic Ocean. Earhart also set the Woman's Transcontinental Speed Record on August 24, 1932, when she flew from Los Angeles, California, to Newark, New Jersey, in record time. That same year Earhart was awarded the American National Geographic Society Award Medal, presented by President Herbert Hoover. In July 1937, during her attempt to fly around the world, her plane was lost over the Pacific Ocean. The bodies of Earhart and her co-pilot, Tom Ninon, have never been found. Since that event numerous theories have been suggested about their fate. Earhart's husband, George Palmer Putnam (whom she married in 1931), released her autobiography, *Last Flight,* the year after her disappearance.

1933 ▪ Frances Perkins appointed U.S. Secretary of Labor

Frances Perkins (1882–1965) was born in Boston, Massachusetts. A longtime civil servant in New York State, Perkins became the first woman cabinet member in the United States when President Franklin D. Roosevelt appointed her Secretary of Labor. She was reappointed for each of his three additional terms in office. During her tenure she drafted the Social Security Act (1935) and the National Labor Relations Act (1935). Perkins later served on the Civil Service Commission under President Harry S Truman.

1933 ▪ Dorothy Day cofounded the *Catholic Worker*

Dorothy Day (1897–1980) was born in Brooklyn, New York. After converting to Roman Catholicism in 1927, she cofounded the monthly publication *Catholic Worker,* which sold for a penny a copy. Influenced by a French priest named Peter Maurin, she started the Catholic Worker Movement and established "houses of hospitality" in urban and rural areas for people struggling to survive during the Great Depression (1929—early 1940s). As a pacifist (antiwar activist) and strong supporter of unionization for farm workers, Day advocated Catholic church involvement in labor and antiwar activities. Her autobiography, *The Long Loneliness,* was published in 1952.

A pacifist and strong supporter of unionization for farm workers, Dorothy Day (middle) advocated Catholic church involvement in labor and antiwar activities.

1934 ▪ Peggy Guggenheim established art gallery

Peggy (Marguerite) Guggenheim (1898–1980) was born in New York City. Her first marriage in 1922 ended in divorce eight years later. Guggenheim lived in Paris, France, until 1941. During that time she socialized with prominent artists and accumulated a collection of paintings. With the support of her friend, artist Marcel Duchamp, she opened the Guggen-

Helped by artist Marcel Duchamp, Peggy Guggenheim opened the Guggenheim-Jeune Art Gallery, which was devoted to modern art.

heim-Jeune Art Gallery, which was devoted to modern art. After the outbreak of World War II (1939–1945) Guggenheim returned to the United States accompanied by artist Max Ernst, whom she married in 1941. Around the same time she founded a New York City gallery called Art of This Century. Having divorced Ernst in 1945, Guggenheim moved to Venice, Italy, after the war. Her home, the Palazzo Venier dei

Leoni on the Grand Canal, now houses the renowned Guggenheim Collection.

1935 ▪ Mary McLeod Bethune founded National Council of Negro Women

Mary McLeod Bethune (1875–1955) was born in Maysville, South Carolina, to former slaves. After teaching in schools in the South, she founded the Daytona Normal and Industrial School for Girls in 1904. The school merged with the Cookman Institute in 1923, becoming Bethune-Cookman College, with Bethune serving as president. In 1935 she founded the National Council of Negro Women, a coalition of national organizations to help improve the status of black women in the United States. Bethune was the organization's first president. During the administration of U.S. president Franklin D. Roosevelt, she was appointed director of the Division of Negro Affairs of the National Youth Administration. Bethune thus became the first African American woman to head an American federal agency.

1935 ▪ Leni Riefenstahl made controversial motion picture

Before embarking on her film directing career, German filmmaker Leni Riefenstahl (born 1902) was a professional dancer and actress. In 1931 Riefenstahl formed her own production company and directed and starred in *The Blue Light.* Three years later she directed the infamous Nazi documentary *Triumph of the Will,* a character study of Nazi leader Adolf Hitler and his frightening grip on the German people during World War II. (The Nazi party was a fanatical racist political party in Germany headed by Hitler.) Riefenstahl was widely criticized on the grounds that she had glorified the Nazi rally at Nuremberg (the city where the party's annual meetings were held). She steadfastly denied any relationship with Hitler, claiming not to have understood the Nazis' genocidal plans (their plans to destroy the entire Jewish population in Europe).

At the end of World War II (1939–1945) Riefenstahl was held by the Allies (British, American, and Russian forces) on suspicion of pro-Nazi activities, but the charges were dismissed. After the war she turned from filmmaking to a career as a photojournalist under the name Helen Jacobs. Riefenstahl published her autobiography, *The Sieve of Time,* in 1992.

c. 1935 ▪ Grandma Moses began painting career

Anna Mary Moses (1860–1961) was born in Washington County, New York. She was interested in art as a child, but she spent most of her life working farms in Virginia and New York with her husband Thomas Moses, whom she married in 1887. When she was about 75 Moses began making detailed primitive paintings of American rural life. (Primitive paintings, also known as folk art, feature simple drawings decorated with bright colors.) Known as "Grandma" Moses by this time, she sold her artwork in a local drug store. In 1938 her paintings were discovered by an art collector and were shown in an exhibition at the Museum of Modern Art the following year. Moses had her first solo exhibition at the age of 80 in New York City.

1936 ▪ Beryl Markham made east-west transatlantic flight

Beryl Markham (1902–1986) was born in England, then moved with her father to East Africa when she was four years old. While growing up among native African children, she learned to speak the Masai and Swahili languages. After working as a horse trainer and breeder for several years, she turned to aviation. Beginning in 1931 she operated a flying service throughout Africa. In 1936 she made a solo flight across the Atlantic Ocean from east to west. After crash-landing in Nova Scotia, she was honored with a ticker-tape parade in New York City. (In 1933, however, Amy Johnson Mollison had flown from Wales to Connecticut, preceding Markham by three years.) While living in California, Markham wrote her well-known autobiography *West with the Night,* which describes her experiences in Africa as well as her love of flying.

1936 ▪ Sally Stearns became coxswain

On May 27, 1936, Sally Stearns became the first woman coxswain (one who steers a racing boat and directs the boat's rowers) of a men's college varsity crew. She led the Rollins College shell ("shell" is the term given to the racing vessel) in a race against Marietta College.

1936 ▪ Margaret Bourke-White became staff photographer

Margaret Bourke-White (1906–1971) was born in New York City. After studying photography at Columbia University she worked as an industrial and architectural photographer. Bourke-White was hired as staff photographer for a new magazine called *Life* in 1936. For the next three decades she photographed the human side of news events. Among her most memorable projects was shooting the opening of the concentration camps (where Jews were imprisoned and executed by the Nazis in Germany) after World War II (1939–1945). She also documented political unrest in Pakistan, India, and South Africa. Bourke-White collaborated with Erskine Caldwell, whom she married in 1939, on an acclaimed book about poverty in the United States, *You Have Seen Their Faces* (1937). Although she was stricken with Parkinson's disease in 1952, she continued to work until 1969. Bourke-White's autobiography, *Portrait of Myself,* was published in 1963.

Margaret Mitchell wrote Gone with the Wind, which won the Pulitzer Prize for literature in 1937.

1936 ▪ Margaret Mitchell published *Gone with the Wind*

Margaret Mitchell (1900–1949) was born in Atlanta, Georgia, where she studied to be a doctor. She became a journalist, however, and in 1926 began working on a novel about the South during the Civil War (1860–1865). Ten years later Mitchell published *Gone with the Wind*. The book won the Pulitzer Prize for literature in 1937, selling over 25 million copies. In 1939 it was made into a major feature film, becoming one of the most successful motion pictures of all time.

1937 ▪ Genora Johnson founded Women's Emergency Brigade

In 1937 Genora Johnson founded the Women's Emergency Brigade (WEB) days after the start of a sit-down strike by the United Auto Workers (UAW) in Flint, Michigan. The duties of the WEB included staffing picket lines around the clock, taking charge of publicity, running a first-aid station, distributing literature, encouraging community support for the strikers, running a day-care center for WEB participants, establishing a welfare committee and a speaker's bureau, and visiting with wives who opposed the strike. The Flint WEB started with 50 women but soon grew to 350 and became the model for similar brigades in other cities where automobiles were manufactured.

1937 ▪ Anne O'Hare McCormick won Pulitzer Prize

American journalist Anne O'Hare McCormick (1881–1954) became the first woman to receive the Pulitzer Prize for distinguished correspondence. She was awarded the prize for her international reporting for the *New York Times* on the rise of Italian fascism. (The fascist movement grew under the leadership of Italian dictator Benito Mussolini throughout the 1920s and 1930s. Fascism is centered on the belief in a certain ethnic group's supremacy over all others. Under a fascist government, all forms of democracy [rule by the people] are destroyed, and opposition to dictatorial rule is suppressed—sometimes violently.) In 1936 McCormick also became the first woman to sit on the *New York Times* editorial board.

1937 ▪ Nadia Boulanger conducted London Orchestra

French musician Nadia Boulanger (1887–1979) was born in Paris. In 1918, after studying voice with her father and other prominent teachers, she began teaching music in her home and at schools in Europe and the United States. In 1937 Boulanger became the first woman to conduct a symphony orchestra in London, England. She was also the first woman to conduct regular concerts with several orchestras in the United States.

1937 ▪ Dorothy Fields won Academy Award

Dorothy Fields (1904–1974) was born in Allenhurst, New Jersey. Her father was Lew Fields, a popular comedian of his era. Dorothy became a lyricist (writer of words for songs), writing several popular songs with composer Jimmy McHugh. In 1937 she won an Academy Award for her lyrics to Jerome Kern's tune "The Way You Look Tonight," which was featured in the 1936 movie *Swing Time*. Fields was the first woman to win an Oscar in this category.

1937 ▪ Margaret Rudkin established Pepperidge Farm

Margaret Fogarty Rudkin (1897–1967) was born in New York City. In 1923 she married Henry Albert Rudkin, and they moved to an estate called Pepperidge in Fairfield, Connecticut. During the Great Depression of the 1930s (a period of severe economic slowdown in the United States) the Rudkins' financial situation became unstable, so Margaret started baking bread to earn an income. According to some accounts, though, she was following a doctor's advice for the treatment of her son's asthma by making bread with only fresh ingredients and no chemical additives. After much trial and error, Rudkin devised a recipe that pleased her family, and she began selling the bread to her local grocer. She established Pepperidge Farm Products (based on the name of their estate), which soon developed into a multimillion-dollar business. Demand for the bread grew quickly, and in 1940 alone Rudkin sold more than 50,000 loaves.

1937 ▪ Zora Neale Hurston wrote *Their Eyes Were Watching God*

African American author Zora Neale Hurston was born on January 7, 1903, in Eatonville, Florida. She graduated from Barnard College in New York City in 1928 and went on to do important research on black folklore in the American South as well as in Haiti and Jamaica. In 1937 Hurston published her best-known novel, *Their Eyes Were Watching God.* Her other works include the novels *Jonah's Gourd Vine* (1934) and *Moses, Man of the Mountain* (1939); the autobiography *Dust*

Zora Neale Hurston was the first woman to successfully combine careers as a cultural anthropologist and accomplished fiction writer.

Tracks on a Road (1942); and the controversial play *Mule Bone: A Comedy of Negro Life* (first produced on Broadway and published in 1991). Hurston was the first woman to successfully combine careers as a cultural anthropologist (one who studies human beings, their relationships, and the ways they live) and an accomplished writer of fiction.

1938 ▪ Katherine Blodgett invented nonreflective glass

Katherine Burr Blodgett (1898–1979) was born in Schenectady, New York. After graduating from Bryn Mawr College she received a master's degree from the University of Chicago. In 1926 she became the first woman to earn a doctorate in physics (the science of matter and energy) at Cambridge University in England. Blodgett was also the first woman to be hired as a scientist by the General Electric Company (GE), where she spent her entire career (1918–1957). Working with Irving Langmuir at the GE plant in Schenectady, she made several significant contributions to the field of industrial chemistry. In 1938 Blodgett invented nonreflective glass, which is now used in camera and optical equipment. During World War II (1939–1945) she made breakthroughs in airplane wing deicing techniques and designed a smoke screen that saved numerous lives in military actions. After the war she developed an instrument that could be placed in weather balloons to measure humidity in the upper atmosphere. Blodgett was awarded the Francis P. Garvan Medal by the American Chemical Society in 1951.

1938 ▪ Patty Berg named Outstanding Female Athlete of the Year

Patty Berg (1918–) was born in Minneapolis, Minnesota. As a teenager she became interested in golf, and by the age of 15 she had entered amateur competitions. In 1938 she was

voted Outstanding Female Athlete of the Year by the Associated Press after she won that year's U.S. Women National Amateur Golf Tournament. Berg had also had nine other victories in 13 tournaments. The first woman golfer to earn over $100,000, Berg turned professional—with the Wilson Company as her corporate sponsor. In 1948 she and several other women golfers, including Mildred "Babe" Zaharias, founded the Ladies Professional Golf Association (LPGA). In 1951 Berg was inducted into the LPGA Hall of Fame. (*Also see entry dated 1932: "Babe" Zaharias won two Olympic gold medals.*)

1938 ▪ Frances Moulton served as bank president

Frances Estelle Mason Moulton was elected president of the Limerick National Bank in Limerick, Maine, to fill the vacancy caused by the death of her father in 1938. Moulton thus became the first woman to serve as president of a U.S. bank.

In 1938 Katherine Blodgett invented nonreflective glass, a product used in camera and optical equipment.

1939 ▪ Harriet Hardy began medical career

Harriet Hardy was born in Arlington, Massachusetts. In 1928 she graduated from Wellesley College and four years later earned a medical degree from Cornell University. In 1939 she accepted a post as college doctor and director of health education at Radcliffe College in Cambridge, Massachusetts. By the early 1940s Hardy was conducting research on a strange respiratory disease that developed among the workers in fluorescent lamp factories in nearby Lynn and Salem, Massachusetts. She found that the cause of the disease was dust or vapor from beryllium (a light metal used in the manufacture of fluorescent lamps) that was being inhaled by factory workers. Hardy became an expert in beryllium poisoning, writing papers that educated and alerted the medical community to its dangers. She also established a registry of berylliosis cases at the Massachusetts General Hospital. This registry later served as a model for the tracking of other occupation-related disorders.

In 1954 Hardy was among the first scientists to identify a link between asbestos (long mineral fibers that at one time were used for insulation) and cancer. Concerned with the effects of radiation on the human body, she worked with the Atomic Energy Commission in Los Alamos, New Mexico, to study radiation poisoning. She made a number of suggestions toward better working conditions in nuclear power plants. In 1955 she was named Woman of the Year by the American Medical Women's Association. Hardy was appointed clinical professor at Harvard Medical School in 1971.

1939 ▪ Madeleine Pelletier arrested for performing abortions

Madeleine Pelletier (1874–1939) was born in Paris, France. Although she left school at the age of 12, she later qualified to become a doctor. Pelletier began practicing medicine when she was 25, becoming one of the first women doctors in Paris in the early twentieth century. She was an outspoken opponent of the French government's push to increase family size (an attempt by government officials to boost the French population), and she began providing women with information on birth control. In 1939 Pelletier was arrested for performing abortions and was committed to a mental hospital, where she died later that year.

1939 ▪ Ethel Waters appeared on Broadway

Ethel Waters (1896–1977) was born in Chester, Pennsylvania. A talented singer, she made her first recording in 1921. By the 1930s she had taken acting roles, and when she appeared in the play *Mamba's Daughters* in 1939 she became one of the first African American women to star on Broadway. Waters went on to a successful film career reprising her roles from the plays *Cabin in the Sky* (1943) and *The Member of the Wedding* (1952), which was written by Carson McCullers. For her role in *Pinky* (1949), a film that focused on the issue of African Americans "passing" as white, she received an Academy Award nomination for best supporting actress. (*Also see entry dated 1940: Carson McCullers published* The Heart Is a Lonely Hunter.)

Photographer Dorothea Lange chronicled the Great Depression with images like White Angel Breadline, San Francisco *(1933).*

1939 ▪ Dorothea Lange documented Great Depression

American photographer Dorothea Nutzhorn Lange (1895–1965) was born in Hoboken, New Jersey. She studied photography at Columbia University with innovative photographer Clarence White. In 1916 she began a career as a society photographer, but she soon turned to more serious work. She took her most famous shots during the Great Depression, photographing sharecroppers and tenant farmers in the American Southwest. (The Great Depression was a period of severe economic hardship in the United States from 1929 to the early 1940s.) In 1939 Lange and her husband, Paul Taylor, published a collection of these photographs titled *An American Exodus: A Record of Human Erosion.* Known for her documentary work, Lange is remembered in particular for her famous pic-

Soviet Women Serve in the Military

During World War II (1939–1945) the Soviet Union put women to work in factories because the men had all been drafted into the military. Unlike other nations, however, more than 800,000 Soviet women were also assigned to combat roles in the armed forces. Although a low percentage of that total number actually fought on the front lines, the integration of women into combat units was unique among nations involved in that war. Women served as artillery personnel, pilots, infantry, engineers, naval personnel, and snipers. Many were highly decorated.

ture "The Migrant Mother." In 1965 her photographs were featured in a one-person show at the Museum of Modern Art in New York City. Lange was the first woman photographer to have such an exhibition.

1939 ▪ Judy Garland played Dorothy in *The Wizard of Oz*

Judy Garland (1922–1969) was born Frances Ethel Gumm in Grand Rapids, Minnesota. As a child she performed in a vaudeville team with her two sisters. (Vaudeville was a form of stage entertainment presented by various performers such as comedians, singers, trained animals, dancers, and acrobats). She changed her name to Judy Garland when she was hired by Metro-Goldwyn-Mayer (MGM) motion picture studios in 1935. During the 1930s and 1940s Garland appeared in several films, including the popular Andy Hardy classics with child actor Mickey Rooney. Her most famous role, however, was that of Dorothy in *The Wizard Of Oz* (1939). Show business took its toll on Garland, though. After years of drug and alcohol abuse, she died at the age of forty-seven. Garland's daughters, Liza Minnelli and Lorna Luft, have also pursued successful stage and film careers.

1940 ▪ Carson McCullers published *The Heart Is a Lonely Hunter*

American author Lula Carson Smith McCullers (1917–1967) was born in Columbus, Georgia. As a child McCullers loved making up stories. When she was just 17 she moved to New York City and worked at odd jobs, saving money to study at Columbia and New York universities. In 1936 McCullers published her first story, "Wunderkind"; she was only 19 years old. In 1940 she wrote *The Heart Is a Lonely Hunter* and became an overnight success in New York.

McCullers is known for her novels and stories about female adolescence and rebellion against traditional gender expectations. Among her other works are *The Member of the Wedding* (1946), which she adapted as a play and later as a film (1952). A motion picture version of McCullers's novella (short novel) *Ballad of the Sad Cafe* (1952) was made in 1991. (*Also see entry dated 1939: Ethel Waters appeared on Broadway.*)

Carson McCullers was known for her novels and stories about female adolescence and rebellion against traditional gender expectations.

1940 ▪ Margaret Chase Smith joined House of Representatives

Margaret Chase (1897–1995) was born in Skowhegan, Maine, where her father was a barber. In 1930 she married Clyde Smith. When her husband died in 1949 she took his seat in the U.S. House of Representatives. Smith went on to serve nine years in the House and 23 years in the U.S. Senate. In 1964 she ran as the Republican Party nominee for U.S. president. Although Smith was not elected, she received 20 delegate votes at the Republican National Convention in San

Francisco. This total was higher than the votes given any other candidate except the winner of the nomination, Senator Barry Goldwater of Arizona. Smith's books include *Gallant Women* (1968) and *Dedication of Conscience* (1972).

1940 ▪ Corrie ten Boom hid Jews from Nazis

Cornelia Arnolda Johanna ten Boom (1892–) was born in Amsterdam, Holland, but grew up in the city of Haarlem. Her parents were Calvinists (people who followed the theological system of French reformer John Calvin). ten Boom was employed as a watchmaker in her father's shop; she was also the first woman in the Netherlands to be licensed as a watchmaker. She and her older sister, Betsie, lived with their father Casper in the rooms above the watch shop. In 1940 Germany invaded Holland, and within months, the "Nazification" of the Dutch people (control by the German Fascist Party under chancellor Adolph Hitler) began. The ten Booms started taking in resistance fighters hiding from the Gestapo (the secret state police) as well as "underdivers" (Dutch Jews and young men wanted by the police). The family also established a network of "safe houses" in the country. Corrie was an overseer of all these operations for four years.

In 1944 the ten Boom home was raided by the Gestapo and the family was arrested. The ten Booms were split up and Casper died ten days later. Corrie and Betsie were eventually shipped to the Ravensbruck concentration camp in Germany, where Betsie died in December, 1944. Two weeks later Corrie was released due to a clerical error. Soon after she left Ravensbruck, the remaining women went to the gas chambers. After the war ten Boom established a training center for evangelical workers. ten Boom published her autobiography, *The Hiding Place*, in 1971.

1942 ▪ Sylvia Porter revealed as financial columnist

From the early 1930s Sylvia Porter, financial reporter for the *New York Post,* had published her financial column anonymously. Her editors believed investors would not respect a woman's advice on money. When Porter's column became wildly popular, the *Post* capitalized on her gender by featuring her photo and byline on the column.

1944 ▪ Anti-Nazi activist Hannah Senesh executed

Hannah Senesh (1921–1944) grew up in a Jewish family in Budapest, Hungary, in the 1930s. During this time the Nazis, led by German chancellor Adolph Hitler, initiated their plan to conquer Europe and annihilate (wipe out) the Jewish people. When Senesh converted to Zionism in 1939, she moved to a kibbutz (a group farm or settlement) in Palestine. At the kibbutz, she was worried about the fate of her widowed mother if Hungary fell to the Nazis. In 1943 Senesh decided to return to her native country and bring her mother to Palestine. She volunteered for a British spy unit that was going into Yugoslavia. In March of 1944, Senesh and three young men parachuted into Yugoslavia, where they worked with partisans (anti-Nazi guerilla fighters). The following June, Senesh and three other comrades crossed into Hungary. They were immediately captured by police, who confiscated Senesh's radio and arrested her. Senesh was sent to Budapest, where she was held in military prisons. In November Senesh was sentenced to death, with no possibility of appeal and no final visit from her mother (who had also been imprisoned). Within a few days Senesh was executed by a firing squad. In 1950, three years after the Jews established the state of Israel, Senesh's body was buried in Haifa with full military honors.

1944 ▪ Martha Gellhorn reported on D-Day invasion

Martha Gellhorn (1908–) was born in St. Louis, Missouri. She became a war correspondent (a journalist who writes reports on the battle scene) in 1937 during the Spanish Civil War (1936–1939). Gellhorn sent her dispatches, which were published in *Collier's* magazine, from Madrid, Spain. She was married to American novelist Ernest Hemingway from 1940 to 1945.

In 1943 Gellhorn began reporting on World War II (1939–1945). On June 6, 1944, she was the only woman journalist to go ashore with Allied (mainly British and American) troops during the D-Day invasion of Normandy, France (a land- and water-based invasion to free France from German occupation). Over the next three decades Gellhorn reported on conflicts in Southeast Asia, the Middle East, and Central America. She ended her career by reporting on the Vietnam war (1954–1975) for the British publication *The Guardian.* Gellhorn also wrote short stories and novels.

1945 ▪ Barbara Castle elected to British Parliament

English journalist Barbara Betts Castle (1910–) was elected a member of the British Parliament in 1945. During the 34 years she served in the House of Commons, Castle held several cabinet positions, including minister of overseas development, minister of transport, and secretary of state for social services. In the 1970s Castle sponsored and pushed through Parliament the Equal Pay Act, which banned gender discrimination in the workplace. In 1979 she became a member of the European Parliament and served as vice chair of the Socialist Group.

1945 ▪ Eva Perón supported women's causes in Argentina

Eva Duarte De Perón (1919–1952) was born into a poor family in Los Toldos, Buenos Aires, Argentina. After a career as an actress she met Argentine president Juan Perón, whom she married in 1945. Known as "Evita," she became a powerful political asset to her husband. Eva supported women's rights issues, founding the Peronista Feminist Party in 1949. As the unofficial minister of health and labor, she worked to improve conditions among the working classes and established the Eva Perón Foundation. After she died of cancer in 1955 her body was stolen from its resting place. The corpse was hidden for nearly 20 years before being brought back to Argentina by Juan Perón's second wife, Isabel, when he died in 1974. Eva Perón's life story provided the basis for *Evita,* a 1978 Broadway musical by Tim Rice and Andrew Lloyd Webber. In 1997 the play was adapted for a film starring songstress Madonna in the title role. (*Also see entry dated 1974: Isabel Perón became president of Argentina; and 1997: Madonna debuted on the pop charts and MTV.*)

1946 ▪ Billie Holiday performed at New York Town Hall

Billie Holiday (1915–1959) was born in Baltimore, Maryland. During the 1930s she sang in clubs in New York City. Becoming famous for her jazz interpretations of popular songs, she made recordings with such well-known musicians as clarinetist Benny Goodman and bandleader Count Basie. In 1946 Holiday performed at Town Hall in New York City, becoming the first female jazz singer to give a solo performance there. Holiday also made several films in the late 1940s, but her career faltered because of her increasing addiction to drugs.

1946 ▪ Mary Ritter Beard published *Women as a Force in History*

American feminist and historian Mary Ritter (1876–1958) was born in Indianapolis, Indiana. In 1900 she married Charles Austin Beard, with whom she collaborated on several publications, including *History of the United States* (1921) and *The Rise of American Civilization* (1927). In 1907 Beard joined the National Women's Trade Union League and organized strikes and protests. Then from 1913 to 1917 she worked for the Congressional Union, which later became the National Women's Party. In 1946 Beard published her landmark piece *Women as a Force in History,* an influential study of the role of women through the ages. Her other publications include *Woman's Work in Municipalities* (1915) and *On Understanding Women* (1931).

1946 ▪ Artist Frida Kahlo received recognition

Frida Kahlo (1907–1954) was born in Coyoacán, Mexico City, Mexico. Her father was a German Jewish immigrant and her mother was a Mexican Catholic. Kahlo wanted to be a doctor, but when she was fifteen she was struck by a bus and seriously injured. While she was recovering, Kahlo began painting

In 1946 Billie Holiday performed at Town Hall in New York City, becoming the first female jazz singer to give a solo performance there.

Anne Frank and her family lived in hiding from the Nazis for over two years.

and sent her work to the painter and muralist Diego Rivera. The couple were married in 1928, beginning a long and troubled relationship. Kahlo continued painting, producing often-shocking pictures with strong colors and surreal (unrealistic) images. In 1940 she entered her work in the International Exhibition of surrealism in Mexico City, and, in 1946, she was awarded a prize at the Annual Exhibition of Fine Arts.

1947 ▪ Anne Frank's diary was published

Anne Frank (1929–1945) was born in Frankfurt-am-Main, Germany, into a Jewish family. In 1933, when the Nazi regime began its anti-Semitic (anti-Jewish) policies, her family fled to Amsterdam, Holland. From 1942 until 1944 the Franks and four other people lived in a concealed back room of an office until they were discovered by the Gestapo (the Nazi police). The family was then transported to the Belsen concentration camp, where Anne died in 1944. After the Nazis were defeated in World War II (1939–1945), Anne's diary was discovered in Amsterdam. The moving, even optimistic account of Anne's experiences during her two years in hiding was published in German in 1947, then translated into English as *The Diary of Anne Frank* in 1952. Anne's story was the basis for a play in 1958 and a film in 1959.

1947 ▪ Edith Ronne landed on Antarctica

Edith Ronne (b. 1919) was a scientist and the wife of Finn Ronne, the Norwegian-American explorer who had made Antarctic expeditions with Admiral Richard Byrd. In 1947 Edith Ronne accompanied her husband on the first expedition to Antarctica that included women. Traveling with them was scientist Jenny Darlington. The party landed at Marguerite Bay, Antarctica, on March 12, 1947. The Ronne Ice Shelf in the Weddell Sea was named for Finn Ronne.

1947 ▪ Dorothy Fuldheim became television news anchor

Dorothy Fuldheim (b. 1893) was a radio newscaster in Cleveland, Ohio, when she became the first female television news anchor in 1947. She received the assignment at WEWS-TV, the first television station in the region between New York and Chicago, Illinois, to go on the air. At first the sponsor, a beer company, was reluctant to underwrite a newscast anchored by a woman. However, the station stood by Fuldheim and the beer company finally relented. Fuldheim remained at the anchor desk for 18 years. During her career she interviewed many notable public figures. By 1979 Fuldheim, who was still anchoring the early newscast, had earned the distinction of being on the job longer than any other television broadcaster—male or female.

1947 ▪ Laura Z. Hobson published novel about anti-Semitism

American writer Laura Zametkin Hobson (1900–1986) was born in New York City. In 1947 she published her best-selling novel about anti-Semitism (anti-Jewish sentiments), *Gentlemen's Agreement.* Among her other works are *The Trespassers* (1943), *The Celebrity* (1951), *First Papers* (1964), and *Consenting Adults* (1975).

1948 ▪ Tilly Edinger originated new theory of evolution

Tilly Edinger was born in Frankfurt am Main, Germany. After attending the universities of Heidelberg and Munich, she received her doctorate in natural philosophy from the University of Frankfurt in 1921. From 1927 to 1938 Edinger was the curator of fossil vertebrates (animals with spinal columns) at the Senckenberg Museum in Frankfurt, a job for which she received no pay. In 1929 she published the groundbreaking study *Die fossilen Gehirne* (title means "Fossil Brains"). Fleeing the anti-Semitism (discrimination against Jews) of the Nazis, Edinger, who was Jewish, went to London, England, in 1939. She later moved to the United States and became a researcher at the Museum of Comparative Zoology at Harvard, where she remained for the rest of her life. Edinger originated the idea that evolution is a complex branching process. In 1948 she published *Evolution of the Horse Brain,* which established that the rates of evolution vary and that as mammals adapt to different environments, various parts of the brain interact differently. Edinger is credited as one of the originators of paleoneurology (the study of the brain through fossil remains).

1948 ▪ Fanny Blankers-Koen won four Olympic gold medals

Fanny Blankers-Koen (b. 1918) was born in Amsterdam, Holland. At the 1948 Summer Olympic games in London, England, she became the first and only woman to win four gold medals in track and field in a single Olympics (100-meter, 200-meter, 80-meter hurdles, and anchor of the 4x100-meter relay). She was named 1948's Female Athlete of the Year by the Associated Press. By the end of her career Blankers-Koen had set 13 world records, earned five European golds, and won 58 Dutch national track and field titles. In 1980 Blankers-Koen was elected into the International Women's Sports Hall of Fame.

1948 ▪ Kamaldevi Chattopadhyay founded Indian Co-operative Union

Kamaldevi Chattopadhyay (b. 1903) was born in India. Following the partition of India and Pakistan in 1947, she saw the need for an organization that would help refugees participate in commercial (moneymaking or business) enterprises. (In August of 1947 India and Pakistan become two separate and independent nations. Pakistan is a predominantly Muslim nation, whereas the Hindu religion is dominant in India. Pakistan's borders were established from territory that was formerly part of India.) Chattopadhyay founded the Indian Co-operative Union, a movement that would promote the making and selling of Indian crafts. In 1952 she helped to found the World Crafts Council.

1948 ▪ Lina Wertmueller joined American studio

Lina Wertmueller (1928–) was born in Rome, Italy. Starting her career as a teacher, she turned to writing, directing, and acting in films. In 1948 she signed an exclusive directing contract with Warner Bros. film studio in Hollywood, California. In 1976 she made *Pasqualino Sette Belleze* ("Seven Beauties"), a movie set in a Nazi concentration camp during World War II. That year Wertmueller was nominated for an Academy Award for best director, becoming the first woman ever to earn a nomination in that category.

1949 ▪ Simone de Beauvoir published *The Second Sex*

Simone de Beauvoir (1908–1986) was born in Paris, France. She studied at the Sorbonne, where she met philosopher and novelist Jean Paul Sartre. As lifelong companions de Beauvoir and Sartre formulated the philosophy of existentialism, which centers on the isolation of the individual's experience in an indifferent and purpose-less world. The pair had a tremendous influence on each other's work. In 1949 de Beauvoir published her landmark book, *Le deuxième sex* (translated and published as *The Second Sex* in 1953). In this study of women in society, de Beauvoir used the phrase "women's liberation" for the first time. She also wrote several novels as well as an autobiography titled *Memoirs of a Dutiful Daughter* (1959).

Simone de Beauvoir used the phrase "women's liberation" for the first time in The Second Sex.

1950 ▪ Beatrice Hicks cofounded Society of Women Engineers

Beatrice Hicks (1919–1979) was born in Orange, New Jersey. She decided to become an engineer at age 13 when her father, an engineer and founder of the Newark Controls Co. in Bloomfield, New Jersey, took her to the Empire State Building and the George Washington Bridge and explained that the structures had been designed by engineers. She received a bachelor's degree in chemical engineering from Newark College of Engineering in 1939 and studied electrical engineering until 1943. In

1945 Hicks joined her father's firm as chief engineer and a year later was named vice president. She also decided to further her education, earning a master's degree in physics (the science of matter and energy) from Stevens Institute of Technology in 1949, the same year she married Rodney Chipp, also an engineer. In 1955 Hicks became president of Newark Controls. She later invented the gas density switch, an essential part of systems using artificial atmospheres. Hicks cofounded the Society of Women Engineers (SWE) and was elected its first president in 1950. She also served as director of the First International Conference of Women Engineers and Scientists, organized by the SWE and held in New York in 1964.

1950 ▪ Althea Gibson played in major tennis tournament

Althea Gibson (b. 1927) was born in Silver, South Carolina. In 1950 she became the first African American to play in a major U.S. Ladies Tennis Association (USLTA) tournament. After that Gibson continued to break racial barriers in international tennis during the 1950s. She was the first African American woman to win at the French Open (1956) and at Wimbledon (1957). In 1960 Gibson began playing professional golf. Her autobiography, *I Always Wanted to Be Somebody,* was published in 1958. Gibson was elected to the Lawn Tennis Hall of Fame in 1971.

1950 ▪ Florence Chadwick swam English Channel

American swimmer Florence Chadwick was born in San Diego, California. In 1950 Chadwick swam from France to England, setting a new record of 13 hours and 20 minutes. She broke the record previously set by Gertrude Ederle by more than an hour. The following year Chadwick swam from England to France. Breaking her own record in 1953 and 1955, Chadwick went on to achieve several other firsts in swimming.

1950 ▪ Kamichika Ichiko started women's reform publication

Japanese feminist Kamichika Ichiko (1888–1981) launched a weekly publication, *Fujin Times,* in 1950. Ichiko

In 1950 Althea Gibson became the first African American to play in a major U.S. Ladies Tennis Association tournament.

used the publication to increase the status of women in Japan. In 1951 she became the chair of the Council for Women and Youth in the Department of Labor. Ichiko served in the House of Representatives in the Diet (Japan's national legislature) from 1953 to 1969. During this time she led a campaign to make prostitution illegal and authored the Anti-Prostitution Act, which passed in 1956.

Marianne Moore was awarded the Pulitzer Prize for poetry in 1952 for Collected Poems.

1951 ▪ Marianne Moore awarded Pulitzer Prize

American poet Marianne Moore (1887–1972) was born in Kirkwood, Missouri, and was educated at colleges in Pennsylvania. She began publishing her poems around 1915, and in 1926 she became the first woman editor of *The Dial,* a literary periodical in New York City. Moore held that post until the magazine ceased publication. Her early verses were collected in volumes titled *Poems* (1921) and *Selected Poems* (1935). Moore was awarded the Pulitzer Prize for poetry in 1952 for *Collected Poems* (1951). A compilation of her essays, *Predilections,* was published in 1955.

1951 ▪ Marguerite Higgins won Pulitzer Prize for Korean War coverage

Marguerite Higgins (1920–1966) was a war correspondent (a journalist who sends reports from the scene of battle) who accompanied the U.S. Marine amphibious landing at Inchon, Korea, during the Korean War (1950–1953) in 1950. The following year she was awarded a Pulitzer Prize for her account of the battle, becoming the first woman awarded a Pulitzer Prize for overseas reporting.

Having been a correspondent since World War II (1939–1945), Higgins also began reporting on the conflict in Vietnam (1954–1975) in 1963. Strongly anti-Communist, she supported U.S. intervention in Vietnam's civil war. (Communism is a system of government in which the state controls the means of production and the distribution of goods. It clashes with the American ideal of capitalism, which is based on private ownership and a free market system. The war in Vietnam pitted the communist North against the noncommunist South; the United States began bombarding the North in 1964, but American forces pulled out in the early 1970s as the North's victory over the South became undeniable.) In her book *Our*

Vietnam Nightmare (1965), Higgins insisted that the United States would be successful in Vietnam if American public opinion in the 1960s did not turn against the war.

1951 ▪ Armi Ratia cofounded Finnish textile design firm

Finnish designer Armi Ratia (1912–1979) cofounded Marimekko, a textile (clothmaking) design firm for which she served as the first managing director. In 1968 Ratia became the first Finnish woman to be awarded the American Neiman Marcus Award in recognition for her art and business success. By 1970 Marimekko—a very successful international business—was exporting to over 20 countries.

1952 ▪ Flannery O'Connor published *Wise Blood*

Mary Flannery O'Connor (1925–1964) was born in Savannah, Georgia. After attending colleges in Georgia and Iowa she began writing novels about Protestant fundamentalism (a religion based on the literal translation of the Bible). Her first novel, *Wise Blood* (1952), set the theme of bizarre and comic human behavior that she continued to pursue throughout her writing career. O'Connor's other novel, *The Violent Bear It Away,* was published in 1960. She is particularly well known for her short stories, which are included in the anthologies *A Good Man Is Hard to Find and Other Stories* (1955) and *Everything That Rises Must Converge* (1965). A collection of her letters, entitled *The Habit of Being: Letters of Flannery O'Connor* (1979) was published posthumously. O'Connor died of lupus, an autoimmune disease (meaning a person's body develops antibodies that damage the body's own tissues) that affects connective tissue, can cause arthritis and skin rashes, and may damage the kidneys, heart, and brain.

1952 ▪ Joan Sutherland joined Royal Opera

Joan Sutherland was born in Sydney, Australia. She studied singing at the Royal College of Music and Opera School in London. Sutherland quickly established herself in the music world as a gifted coloratura soprano. (Soprano is the name given to the highest singing voice of women; coloratura is a type of soprano that is very theatrical and elaborate.) In 1952 she joined the Royal Opera, making her debut as the First Lady in *The Magic Flute* by Austrian composer Wolfgang Amadeus Mozart. Sutherland married her accompanist and coach Richard Bonynge. Soon gaining an international reputation, she sang a wide range of roles and returned to Australia in 1965 with her own opera company. Sutherland was named a Dame of the British Empire upon her retirement in 1991.

1952 ▪ Rosalind Franklin helped determine structure of DNA

Rosalind Franklin (1920–1958) was born in London, England. After studying chemistry at Cambridge University, she worked as a researcher for the British Coal Utilization Research Association. Her specialty was carbon fiber technology. Franklin later moved to Paris, France, where she conducted research in X-ray crystallography (the use of X rays to determine the structure of a crystal). Upon returning to London in 1951, she joined the research staff at King's College. The following year she recorded the existence of a form of deoxyribonucleic acid, commonly known as DNA. (DNA is a long, chainlike molecule in the nucleus of most living cells that carries the genetic—or hereditary—material in all organisms.)

Franklin's work provided the scientific evidence upon which American biologist James Watson and British physicist Francis Crick based their double-helix molecular model of DNA. When Watson and Crick were awarded the Nobel Prize in 1962, Franklin received no recognition for her discovery. (The Nobel committee honors only living recipients, and Franklin had died of cancer four years earlier.) Ten years later Watson noted in his book *The Double Helix* that he realized "years too late the struggle that the intelligent woman faces to be accepted [in] the scientific world."

1953 ▪ Marilyn Monroe became a sex symbol

Marilyn Monroe (1926–1962) was born Norma Jean Baker in Los Angeles, California. She grew up in foster homes because her mother's mental illness made her an unfit parent. During World War II (1939–1945), while working at an airplane factory, Baker was "discovered" by a photographer who put her picture on the cover of *Yank* magazine. After taking the screen name "Marilyn Monroe," she appeared in small parts until she was hired by Twentieth-Century Fox. In 1953 Monroe starred in three big-budget color films: *Niagara, Gentlemen Prefer Blondes,* and *How to Marry a Millionaire.* She became an international sensation as a blonde bombshell. Such films as *The Seven-Year Itch* (1955) and *Some Like It Hot* (1959) emphasized her talent for comedy, but she also had more serious roles in *Bus Stop* (1956) and *The Misfits* (1961). Monroe was married to baseball player Joe Di Maggio and playwright Arthur Miller, both of whom she divorced. She died of an apparent drug overdose.

Marilyn Monroe became an international sensation with films such as Some Like It Hot *and* Bus Stop.

1953 ▪ Unionist Odessa Komer joined the UAW

Unionist Odessa Komer (1925–) became a member of United Automobile Workers (UAW) Union Local 228 when she went to work as an assembler at Ford Motor Company in Michigan. Soon after joining the union Komer was elected to numerous union positions: she served as an executive board member (1956–58), a member of the District Committee (1958–65), a delegate to the Ford Council and Sub Council 5 (1961–67), and a delegate to the 1964 and 1966 constitutional conventions. She was also a member of the by-laws committee and served as the education chair. Komer was the first woman to hold any of these positions.

1953 ▪ Joan Maud Littlewood founded theater workshop

Joan Maud Littlewood (b. 1914) was born in London, England, where she graduated from the Royal Academy of Dramatic Art. Littlewood and her husband, singer and writer

Ewan McColl, founded the Theatre Union, followed by the Theatre of Action. Littlewood encouraged experimental drama and became one of the most influential stage directors working in England after World War II (1939–1945). She is best known for staging working-class plays such as *The Quare Fellow* (1956), *Fings Ain't Wot They Used T' Be* (1959), and *Oh, What a Lovely War!* (1963). Littlewood's autobiography, *Joan's Book,* was published in 1994.

1953 ▪ Tenley Albright won World Figure Skating Championship

On February 15, 1953, Tenley Albright became the first American woman to win the World Figure Skating Championship.

1953 ▪ Margaret Sanger founded International Planned Parenthood Federation

Margaret Higgins (1883–1966) was born in Corning, New York. She married William Sanger in 1902. While working as a nurse in 1914 Sanger started the magazine *The Woman Rebel,* which gave advice on contraception (birth control). Two years later she opened one of the country's first birth control clinics in New York City. Sanger then organized the first American Birth Control Conference, also in New York City. In 1953 she founded and served as first president of the International Planned Parenthood Federation. Among Sanger's books are *What Every Mother Should Know* (1917) and *My Fight for Birth Control* (1931).

1953 ▪ Oveta Culp Hobby appointed secretary of Health, Education, and Welfare

Texas lawyer and newspaperwoman Oveta Culp Hobby (1905–1995) worked for the War Department and helped in the education of a women's army corps (an organized subdivision of the military). She was appointed colonel of the Women's Army Auxiliary Corps (WAACS) and retained her position in the corps when it changed to the Women's Army Corps (WACS) in 1943. In 1953 President Dwight D. Eisenhower appointed Hobby the first secretary of Health, Education and Welfare, a position she held until 1955.

1953 ▪ Elizabeth II of England was crowned queen

Elizabeth Alexandra Mary Windsor (1926–) is the daughter of King George VI and Lady Bowes-Lyon (now known as the Queen Mother). Elizabeth married Philip Battenburg (now Prince Philip) in 1947. In 1953, after the death of her father, she assumed the British throne as Elizabeth II amidst worldwide celebration. She became the ruler of Great Britain, Northern Ireland, Canada, Australia, and New Zealand. Although Elizabeth has been popular with the British people throughout her long reign, she has encountered several problems. For one thing, contemporary British society is growing more and more discontent with the existence—and expense—of a monarchy. In addition, the marital problems of her children—Prince Charles (the Prince of Wales), Princess Anne, and Prince Andrew— have cast a shadow over the dignity and grandeur expected of the royal family.

1953 ▪ Maureen Connolly won Grand Slam of tennis

Maureen Connolly (1934–1969) was born in San Diego, California. In 1953, at the age of 19, she won the Australian, French, American, and British tennis titles, becoming the first woman to win the Grand Slam of tennis (the term given to the winning of the four major titles in tennis). She went on to win three U.S. titles between 1951 and 1953, as well as three Wimbledon titles (1952, 1953, and 1954). Shortly after winning her last Wimbledon championship Connolly broke her leg in a riding accident and was forced to retire from tennis.

1954 ▪ Dorothy Dandridge nominated for Academy Award

African American actress Dorothy Dandridge (1922–1965) began her career singing in nightclubs and pursuing small screen roles. By the 1950s she had become an African American sex symbol and was referred to as the "Sepia Beauty of the American Screen." (Both of Dandridge's

parents were of mixed racial origin.) In 1954 Dandridge became the first person of color nominated for an Academy Award as best actress. (The nomination was for her role in *Carmen Jones*.) Among her other well-known films are *Island in the Sun* (1957) and *Porgy and Bess* (1959).

Some film historians believe that the deep racial divide existing in the United States in the 1950s kept Dandridge from becoming the huge star she deserved to be. Although she struggled for acceptance as a gifted black dramatic actress, she was type-cast in the role of the "tragic mulatto." Drinking and drug abuse clouded the last few years of her life. Her autobiography, *Everything and Nothing: The Dorothy Dandridge Story,* was published in 1970, five years after her death from a probable drug overdose.

1954 ▪ Sono Ayako became popular Japanese writer

Japanese writer Sono Ayako (1931–) gained prominence with the story "Enrai no kyakutachi" (1954; "Guests from Across the Sea"), which described U.S. military occupation forces. Ayako was recognized as an eloquent narrator who analyzed Japanese society from the perspective of an intellectual, Catholic woman.

1955 ▪ Eloise R. Giblett began groundbreaking genetic studies

Eloise Rosalie Giblett (1921–) was born in Tacoma, Washington. She received a bachelor's degree from the University of Washington in Seattle in 1942. World War II (1939–1945) interrupted her studies for a time, and she served as a medical technician. With the help of the G.I. Bill, Giblett was able to finish her formal education, receiving a master's degree in microbiology from the University of Washington in

1947 and a medical degree from the University of Washington Medical School in 1951.

In 1955 Giblett became a professor of medicine at the University of Washington and an associate director of the Puget Sound Blood Center. For the next 30 years she worked as a researcher, educator, and administrator. Perhaps her most notable achievement was the discovery in the mid–1970s that deficiencies of various enzymes (substances produced by the body that cause certain chemical reactions to occur) can cause inherited immune system disorders. These defects may be curable by gene therapy, and Giblett pointed the way for such research. Giblett also did important research in blood group antibodies. She received the Emily Cooley Award in 1975, the Karl Landsteiner Award in 1976, and the Philip Levine Award from the American Association of Clinical Pathologists in 1978.

The "Whirly Girls"

The "Whirly Girls" was an association of American female helicopter pilots. When the group formed in 1955, there were only 13 licensed female helicopter pilots in the world. The first woman licensed to pilot a helicopter was American aviator Ann Shaw Carter, who received her helicopter rating in 1947.

1955 ▪ Mary Quant opened "Bazaar" in London

Mary Quant (1934–) was born in London, England, where she studied art. In 1955 she and two partners opened a shop called "Bazaar" in the Chelsea area of London to sell their own clothing designs. Two years later Quant married one of her partners, Alexander Plunkett Greene. Their Bazaar became so popular that within less than a decade it expanded into a multimillion-dollar enterprise, playing a central role in the "swinging Britain era." Quant's influence over young women's fashions soon spread worldwide. Among her innovations were the miniskirt and the "wet look" (a fashion experiment in close-fitting vinyl clothing). During the 1970s Quant also sold cosmetics and designed textiles.

1955 ▪ Giuliana Benetton founded knitwear company

Giuliana Benetton (c. 1938–) was the founder and first president of Benetton, the world's largest knitwear company.

In 1955 Rosa Parks was arrested when she refused to give up her seat to a white passenger on a bus in Montgomery, Alabama.

She located the business in Treviso, Italy, the town near Venice where she grew up. By 1986 the company operated 4,000 outlets in 54 countries and had become the world's largest manufacturer of knitwear and the greatest consumer of virgin wool (wool that has no impurities or stains).

1955 ▪ Marian Anderson appeared at Metropolitan Opera

Marian Anderson (1902–1993) was born in Philadelphia, Pennsylvania. In 1955 she became the first African American woman soloist to sing on the stage of the Metropolitan Opera House in New York City. Anderson began singing at age six in her church choir. Her solo career was launched when she was selected over 300 other singers in a contest and given the opportunity to sing with the New York Philharmonic Orchestra. She then toured Europe from 1925 to 1933, receiving rave reviews. In 1939 she was prevented from singing at Constitution Hall in Washington, D.C., because of her race. In protest, U.S. first lady Eleanor Roosevelt arranged for Anderson to give a concert in front of the Lincoln Memorial to an audience of 75,000 people. President Dwight D. Eisenhower appointed Anderson a delegate to the United Nations in 1958, and she received the President's Medal of Freedom in 1963. Anderson published her autobiography, *My Lord, What a Morning,* in 1956. (*Also see entry dated 1929: Eleanor Roosevelt became "ambassadress."*)

1955 ▪ Rosa Parks arrested in Montgomery, Alabama

Civil rights pioneer Rosa Parks (1913–) was born in Tuskegee, Alabama, and for most of her life she worked as a seamstress. In 1955 Parks was arrested when she refused to give up her seat to a white passenger on a bus in Montgomery, Alabama. On the first day of her trial African Americans in Montgomery—led by civil rights activist Martin Luther King,

Jr.—organized a boycott of the city bus system. Considered the beginning of the American civil rights movement, this action led to the 1956 Supreme Court decision declaring bus segregation to be unconstitutional. Parks moved to Detroit, Michigan, in 1957 and remains active in civil rights issues.

1956 ▪ Maria Atanassova flew for commercial airline

Maria Atanassova was the first female pilot to work for a commercial airline. She was made a full pilot for the Soviet airline Aeroflot in 1956. Atanassova caused a sensation when she landed at Heathrow Airport in London, England, in 1966: it was the first time a woman had piloted a large jet aircraft at an airport outside of Russia.

1956 ▪ Bette Nesmith Graham invented "Liquid Paper"

Bette Nesmith Graham (1924–1980) was born in Dallas, Texas. While working as a secretary in the 1950s, Graham recognized the need for a quick method for correcting typing errors. Having no formal training in chemistry, she experimented in her own kitchen with formulations to make quick-drying fluid that would completely cover letters on a page. In 1956 she invented "Liquid Paper" and applied for a patent. Graham offered her invention to International Business Machines (IBM), but the company decided not to market her product. As a result she began selling "Liquid Paper" locally herself, filling the bottles in her garage with the help of her son Michael (who gained fame in the late 1960s as one of *The Monkees* on television). In 1979 Graham sold "Liquid Paper" to the Gillette Corporation for $47.5 million plus royalties.

1957 ▪ Sarah Caldwell established the Boston Opera Company

American conductor Sarah Caldwell (1928–) was born in Maryville, Missouri, and attended the New England Conservatory of Music. She taught at the Berkshire Music Center from 1948 to 1952, then headed the Opera Workshop Department at Boston University from 1952 to 1960. In 1957 Caldwell established the Boston Opera Company, and 19 years later she became the first woman to conduct the orchestra at the Metropolitan Opera House in New York City. Caldwell also served as artistic director of the New Opera Company of Israel.

1957 ▪ Ethel Andrus founded AARP

Former teacher Ethel Andrus (1884–1967) was the founder and first president of the American Association of Retired Persons (AARP). By the 1990s AARP was a powerful lobbying group on issues of importance to retired Americans. (Lobbyists work to influence the votes of legislators on specific issues.) Before she founded AARP, Andrus had also been the founder and first president of the National Retired Teachers Association (NRTA), which was established in 1947.

1957 ▪ Chien-Shiung Wu conducted an important experiment

Nuclear physicist Chien-Shiung Wu (1912–) was born in Shanghai, China. After studying at the University of California at Berkeley, she joined the school's faculty in 1946. Wu conducted an important experiment on beta decay (a radioactive nuclear transformation) in 1957, the year she attained the rank of professor. Her discovery confirmed a prediction made a year earlier by two male colleagues regarding the conservation of parity (the basic symmetry of nature) in reactions involving the weak force of a nucleus. Many believed that Wu should have shared in the 1957 Nobel Prize for physics that was awarded to her two male colleagues, but she was not included among the recipients.

1958 ▪ Kirsten Flagstad directed Norwegian state opera

Soprano Kirsten Malfrid Flagstad (1895–1962) was born in Hamar, Norway. (Soprano is the name given to the highest singing voice of women.) After studying singing in Sweden and Norway, she made her operatic debut in 1913. For the next 20 years she performed throughout Scandinavia, becoming famous for roles in operas by German composer Richard Wagner. Flagstad was the first director of the Norwegian State Opera in Oslo, serving in that capacity from 1958 until 1960. In 1935 she also became the first woman to sing the demanding roles of Sieglinde, Isolde, and Brunnhilde in operas by Wagner at the Metropolitan Opera in New York City.

1958 ▪ **Marion E. Kenworthy became president of American Psychoanalytic Association**

American psychiatrist Marion E. Kenworthy (1891–1980), who had been the first woman professor of psychiatry at Columbia University, became the first woman president of the American Psychoanalytic Association in 1958. (Psychoanalysis is a method of treating emotional disorders by examining the experiences of the past—especially the impact of childhood and of dreams—and their effect on a person's later life.)

1958 ▪ **Maria-Teresa de Filippis drove in Grand Prix auto race**

Italian driver Maria-Teresa de Filippis was the first woman to compete in a modern European Grand Prix auto race.

1958 ▪ **Singer Miriam Makeba gained fame**

Miriam Makeba (1932–) was the first black woman from South Africa to gain an international reputation as a singer. Credited with introducing African songs to the West, she was acclaimed for her performance in the anti-apartheid (anti-segregation) film *Come Back Africa* in 1958. After that—with encouragement from African American folk singer and actor Harry Belafonte—Makeba had several hit records in the United States. She also took an active role in the American civil rights movement of the 1960s. After marrying African American civil rights leader Stokely Carmichael, Makeba settled in African Guinea in the 1970s.

Miriam Makeba was the first black woman from South Africa to gain an international reputation as a singer.

1959 ▪ **Lorraine Hansberry completed *A Raisin in the Sun***

African American playwright Lorraine Hansberry (1930–1965) was born in Chicago, Illinois. After attending the

University of Wisconsin and the School of Art Institute in Chicago, Hansberry gained success a playwright. Her first completed work, *A Raisin in the Sun,* won the New York Drama Critics Circle Award in 1959. The first Broadway play written by an African American woman, *A Raisin in the Sun* focuses on a black family struggling to live their lives in a predominantly white society. Among Hansberry's other works was the play *The Sign in Sidney Brunstein's Window* (1964). After her death her husband published her prose writings in *To Be Young, Gifted and Black: Lorraine Hansberry in Her Own Words* (1969).

1959 ▪ Judith Hart elected to British Parliament

British public official Constance Mary Judith Ridehalgh (1924–1991) was born in Burnley, Lancashire, England. Known professionally as Judith Hart, she was a founder of the Campaign for Nuclear Disarmament. In 1959 she was elected to Parliament as a Labour candidate. During the 1960s she held several ministerial posts, including minister of social security and minister of state for overseas development. Hart also campaigned for an end to apartheid (racial segregation) in South Africa. Appointed Dame of the British Empire in 1979, she retired from Parliament in 1987.

1959 ▪ Shirley Muldowney was professional drag racer

American drag racer Shirley Muldowney (1940–) was born in Burlington, Vermont. A high school dropout, she began her professional racing career in 1959. Driving a pink race car and wearing hot-pink uniforms, Muldowney was at first regarded as a curiosity on the dragster circuit. She has survived a number of life-threatening crashes to beat top-rated drivers in a male-dominated sport. Muldowney was the first woman to qualify for the top competition in hot rod (modified automobile) racing. In 1975 she competed in the supercharged, nitro-burning, unlimited AA-fuel dragster category. In 1977, 1980, and 1982 she won the National Hot Rod Association world championship.

SHIRLEY
MULDOWNEY

Shirley Muldowney was once regarded as a curiosity on the dragster circuit because she drove a pink race car and wore hot-pink uniforms.

1959 ▪ Ruth Handler created Barbie Doll

The "Barbie Doll," created by Ruth Handler, was introduced in 1959 by Mattel, an American toy manufacturer. The fashion doll, her extensive wardrobe, and accessories (including a "Dream House") quickly became a big hit with young girls. In recent years Barbie's continued success has led to worldwide licensing, clothing offshoots, and specialty stores.

At the 1960 summer Olympics in Rome, Italy, Wilma Rudolph became the first woman to win three gold medals in a single Games.

1960 ▪ Wilma Rudolph won three Olympic gold medals

African American runner Wilma Rudolph (1940–1994) was born in Clarksville, Tennessee, into a family of 22 children. She overcame childhood polio (an infectious viral disease) to become a successful high school basketball player and track star. At the 1960 summer Olympic Games in Rome, Italy, Rudolph became the first woman to win three gold medals at a single Olympics. She won the gold in the 100-meter, 200-meter, and relay events. Rudolph was inducted into the U.S. Olympic Hall of Fame in 1983 and the National Women's Hall of Fame in 1994.

1960 ▪ Diane Arbus reached peak of her career

Photographer Diane Arbus (1923– 1971) was born in New York City and was married to fellow photographer Allan Arbus from 1941 to 1969. Starting as a commercial photographer, she eventually rebelled against her upper-class upbringing and concentrated on photographing members of the less-privileged segments of American society. Her work achieved critical and popular acclaim through the 1960s.

1961 ▪ Harper Lee won Pulitzer Prize

American author Harper Lee (1926–) was born in Alabama. She won the Pulitzer Prize in 1961 for her only novel, *To Kill a Mockingbird* (1960). In the story a six-year-old girl named Scout tells the story of her father, a Southern white lawyer named Atticus Finch who defends a black man against charges of raping a white woman. Lee was the first woman to win the Pulitzer Prize since 1942. *To Kill a Mockingbird* was adapted for film in 1962. Featuring Gregory Peck as Finch, the motion picture earned critical acclaim and now stands as a classic of American cinema.

Harper Lee won a Pulitzer Prize in 1961 for her only novel, To Kill a Mockingbird.

1961 ▪ Jerrie M. Cobb passed astronaut tests

American aviator Jerrie M. Cobb was the first of 14 women to qualify to become an astronaut.

1962 ▪ Joy Adamson started World Wildlife Fund

Friederike Gessner Adamson (1910–1980) was born in Troppau, Silesia (now Opava in the Czech Republic), to Austrian parents. After failed marriages to Viktor von Klarwill, an Austrian businessman, and Peter Bally, a botanist who renamed her "Joy," she married George Adamson, a warden with the Kenya game department, in 1943. Joy Adamson's career as a professional conservationist began in 1956 when George shot a lioness that had attacked him. He brought the lioness's three cubs home. Joy wanted to take care of all three of them, but the couple ended up sending two cubs to a zoo.

Naming the third cub Elsa, Adamson tried to raise her so she could return to the wild. Elsa eventually joined a pride (family of lions), mated, and had six cubs of her own. Adam-

son's experiences with Elsa led her to found the World Wildlife Fund in the United States in 1962. She was perhaps best known, however, for her books about Elsa: *Born Free* (1960), which became the basis for a feature film; *Elsa* (1961); *Forever Free* (1962); and *Elsa and Her Cubs* (1965). Adamson was murdered in her home in Kenya in 1980.

1962 ▪ Margot Fonteyn began dancing with Rudolf Nureyev

Margot Fonteyn (1919–1991) was born in Reigate, England. After studying with Irish ballet dancer Ninette de Valois, she joined the Vic-Wells Ballet, the company with which she spent her entire career. (Vic-Wells Ballet eventually became Sadler's Wells Ballet, and finally the Royal Ballet.) Creating roles with Valois and choreographer Frederick Ashton, Fonteyn rose to the position of premier dancer of the Royal Ballet. In 1955 she married Roberto Emilio Arias, the Panamanian ambassador to the Court of St. James in London. In

1962, at the age of 43, she began her celebrated partnership with the great Russian ballet dancer Rudolph Nureyev. Fonteyn also wrote and produced *The Magic of Dance,* a television series; she published her autobiography in 1975.

1962 ▪ Biochemist Gertrude Elion discovered Imuram

American biochemist Gertrude Belle Elion (1918–) was born in New York City. Before World War II (1939–1945) she taught high school. At the beginning of the war, however, she became a researcher at Burroughs Wellcome laboratories. In 1962 Elion developed Imuram, a drug that helped prevent transplant patients from rejecting newly transplanted organs. She patented a total of 45 drug treatments during her career, many with her collaborator, biochemist Dr. George Hitchings.

In 1962 Gertrude Elion developed Imuram, a drug that helped prevent transplant patients from rejecting newly transplanted organs.

1962 ▪ Madeleine L'Engle published *A Wrinkle in Time*

American children's author Madeleine L'Engle (b. 1918) was born in New York City. As a child she attended a series of boarding schools, an unhappy experience that provided the basis for her first novel, *The Small Rain.* L'Engle is best known, however, for *A Wrinkle in Time* (1962), the story of Meg, a girl who has a gift of extrasensory perception (ESP; the ability to predict events before they happen). The book won the 1963 Newbery Medal. Other well-known works by L'Engle include *A Wind in the Door* (1973) and *A Swiftly Tilting Planet* (1978). In all of her writings L'Engle combines elements of fiction and fantasy with themes of family love and moral responsibility.

1963 ▪ Margaret B. Davis developed new theory

Margaret B. Davis (1931–) was born in Boston, Massachusetts. She graduated from Radcliffe College in 1953 with a

During her husband's administration, Jacqueline Kennedy Onassis supervised the restoration of the White House.

bachelor's degree in biology. While at Radcliffe she took courses from noted paleobotanist Elso Borghoorn. (A paleobotanist is a scientist who studies fossil plants.) After obtaining a doctorate in biology from Harvard University in 1957, she pursued research in the new field of palynology (the study of pollen and spores). In 1961 Davis became a researcher in the botany department at the University of Michigan. Two years later she attracted international attention with a paper on a theory of pollen analysis published in the *American Journal of Science*. Davis challenged the prevailing scientific idea that plant and animal communities tend to move unchanged to new locations as the climate changes. By studying pollen from ancient plants she reconstructed past plant communities and showed how they had changed in response to variations in climate or other environmental influences. Davis is the recipient of numerous honors, including the Eminent Ecologist Award and the Nevada Medal.

1963 ▪ Jacqueline Kennedy led the United States in mourning

American first lady Jacqueline Kennedy Onassis (was born in Southampton, Long Island, to a wealthy Roman Catholic family. She worked as a news photographer in Washington, D.C., before marrying John F. Kennedy in 1953. After her husband was elected president of the United States in 1960, she achieved unparalleled fame as first lady. Kennedy supervised the restoration of the White House, and her elegance and style captivated the world. In the aftermath of President Kennedy's assassination in 1963, her grace and poise set the tone for the nation in mourning its slain leader. Jacqueline Kennedy married Aristotle Onassis, a Greek shipping magnate, in 1968. She worked as an editor in New York until her death in 1994.

1963 ▪ Katharine Graham took over *Washington Post*

Publisher Katharine Meyer Graham (1917–) was born in New York City, the daughter of newspaper publisher and financier Eugene Meyer. Beginning her career as a journalist in San Francisco, she joined her father's newspaper in 1939. She married Philip Graham the following year, and in 1948 the couple bought the newspaper. After her husband's suicide in 1963, Graham inherited the Washington Post Company and took over as a forceful manager of the *Washington Post* newspaper. In 1971 she published the controversial "Pentagon Papers" (government documents that revealed the extent of U.S. involvement in the Vietnam conflict), which put the paper at the risk of being sued.

A year later Graham made waves with the paper's coverage of the Watergate scandal (a story that the *Post* uncovered first). (The Watergate scandal involved attempts by the Republican Party to break into the offices of the Democratic Party at the Watergate Hotel in Washington.) In 1974, as a result of her strong leadership, Graham became the first woman to be named to the board of the Associated Press (a news organization). She was appointed president and chief executive officer of the Washington Post Company in 1991. Graham published her autobiography, *Personal History,* in 1997.

A Girl Plays Small-Fry Baseball

Nancy Lotsey joined the New Jersey Small-Fry League and became its first girl player. Due in part to her pitching and batting skills, Lotsey's team won the 1963 championship.

1963 ▪ Helen Bryant established Afro-American Total Theater Arts Foundation

Helen Bryant (1939–1983) founded and served as first president of the Afro-American Total Theater Arts Foundation in New York. Five years later she founded the Richard Allen Center of Culture and Art in New York.

1963 ▪ Betty Friedan published *The Feminine Mystique*

American feminist (women's rights activist) Betty Goldstein Friedan (1921–) was born in Peoria, Illinois. She was

Betty Friedan (center)
began her writing career
by publishing articles
about women's growing
dissatisfaction with
their lives.

educated at Smith College before becoming a homemaker and mother. Friedan began her writing career by publishing articles in magazines about women's growing dissatisfaction with their lives. In 1963 she wrote *The Feminine Mystique,* in which she analyzed the role of women in American society. The book became a bestseller. Friedan founded the National Organization for Women (NOW) in 1966, but she also warned women about the dangers of trying to compete against men. She published her autobiography, *It Changed My Life,* in 1977 and *The Second Stage,* an analysis of the feminist movement, in 1981.

1963 ▪ Sylvia Plath wrote *The Bell Jar*

American writer Sylvia Plath (1932–1963) was born in Boston, Massachusetts. She was educated at Smith College, then was awarded a Fulbright scholarship to Cambridge University in England, where she met her husband, poet Ted Hughes. In 1963 Plath published her autobiographical novel

The Bell Jar under the name Victoria Lucas. The novel featured an account of her painful experiences during a summer as an editor of a chic women's magazine in New York City. Later that year Plath—who was by this time separated from her husband—committed suicide in London. Poems by Plath were published in *Ariel* (1965) and *Collected Poems* (1981), which won the Pulitzer Prize in 1982.

1963 ▪ Barbara Tuchman won her first Pulitzer Prize

Author and historian Barbara Wertheim Tuchman (1912–) was born in New York City. In 1963 she became the first woman to receive the Pulitzer Prize for general nonfiction for her book *The Guns of August,* which recounted the early days of World War I (1914–1918). In 1972 Tuchman received a second Pulitzer Prize for her book *Stilwell and the American Experience in China, 1911–1945* (1971), about the career of U.S. general Joseph W. Stilwell. Seven years later she was elected the first female president of the American Academy and Institute of Arts and Letters.

1963 ▪ Cosmonaut Valentina Tereshkova orbited Earth

Soviet cosmonaut Valentina Tereshkova (1937–) was born in Maslennikovo, Yaroslavl, the daughter of a farmer. Tereshkova was working in a cotton mill when she took up parachuting in her spare time. She was selected for cosmonaut training for the Soviet space program in 1962. A year later she became the first woman (and the tenth person) to orbit Earth 45 times. Tereshkova, who was the solo pilot on the *Vostock 6* space capsule, traveled 1,242,800 miles during her orbital journey. After retiring from the cosmonaut corps she began a long political career in 1966, serving on the Russian Association of International Cooperation at the time of her retirement in 1992. Tereshkova's autobiography, *Valentina: First Woman in Space,* was published in 1993.

1963 ▪ Maria Goeppert-Mayer won Nobel Prize

German-born American physicist Maria Gertrude Goeppert-Mayer (1906–1972) was born in Kattowitz, Germany

Maria Goeppert-Mayer won the Nobel Prize for physics after developing a model for the structure of atomic nuclei.

(now Poland). In 1963 Goeppert-Mayer won the Nobel Prize for physics after developing a model for the structure of atomic nuclei. She shared the prize with physicists Eugene Paul Wigner and Hans Jensen. Goeppert-Mayer had set forth a more sophisticated model of nuclear shells than had previously been available to physicists.

1964 ▪ Sonia Delaunay had retrospective exhibit at Louvre

Sonia Terk Delaunay (1885–1979) was born in Gradizhsk in the Russian Ukraine and grew up in St. Petersburg. She studied drawing at the University at Karlsruhe, Germany, and moved to Paris in 1905. Influenced by French painters Paul Gauguin and Henri Matisse, Delaunay worked with dazzling colors and juxtaposed dark outlines with exotic patterning. In 1964 a retrospective exhibit (a selection of paintings over an entire career) of Delaunay's paintings was held at the Louvre Museum in Paris. Delaunay became the only living woman artist to enjoy a retrospective exhibition at the Louvre.

1964 ▪ Dorothy Crowfoot Hodgkin won Nobel Prize

English chemist Dorothy Crowfoot Hodgkin (1910–) was born in Cairo, Egypt, of British parents. After entering Somerville College for Women at Oxford University in England, she considered becoming an archaeologist. Instead she returned to her lifelong interest in chemistry and crystallography (the science that deals with the forms and structures of crystals) at Somerville College for Women at Oxford University. After graduating from Oxford in 1932, she worked as a researcher in crystallography at Cambridge University and five years later married Thomas Hodgkin, with whom she had three children. During World War II (1939–1945) Hodgkin conducted research on the structure of penicillin, and in 1948 she began groundbreaking work on the structure of vitamin B–12.

Hodgkin is remembered for beginning a new era in science by employing X-ray crystallography to determine the structures of large biochemical molecules. After the war she helped form the International Union of Crystallography, which was instrumental in bringing crystallographers from communist countries into the American and European scientific community. Her activities caused the U.S. government some concern, however, and a travel restriction was placed on her visa. (The restriction was finally lifted in 1990 after the Soviet Union disbanded.) In 1964 Hodgkin won the Nobel Prize in chemistry in recognition of her discoveries of the molecular structures of vitamin B–12, insulin, and penicillin. During her later years she worked with the Pugwash Conference on Science and World Affairs, a scientific organization dedicated to world peace.

1964 ▪ Shirley Williams elected to British Parliament

Shirley Vivien Teresa Brittain Williams (1930–) was born in Chelsea, England, the daughter of British writer Vera Brittain. Williams was one of the most prominent women in British government from the 1960s through the mid–1980s. In 1964 she won a seat in British Parliament as a Labour candidate. During the 15 years she served, she held several ministerial posts in Parliament and worked for comprehensive education guidelines and restrictions on divorce and abortion. Widely regarded as a brilliant political economist and an independent thinker, Williams was a strong voice for her country's membership in the European Economic Community, even when her own party opposed it. In 1981 she helped found the Social Democrat Party and was elected to Parliament again, but she was defeated in 1983. Williams moved to the United States five years later to take a position as professor of politics at the John F. Kennedy School of Government at Harvard University.

1964 ▪ Donna Mae Mins won Sports Car Club of America championship

Donna Mae Mins became the first woman to win a Sports Car Club of America (SCCA) championship, having beaten out 31 men in the Class II production category for imported two-seat sports cars.

1964 ▪ Swimmer Donna de Varona won gold medal

American swimmer Donna de Varona (1947–) was the first woman to win an Olympic gold medal in the 400-meter individual medley event. Varona achieved this record at the summer Olympics in Tokyo, Japan, in 1964, the first year the individual medley was open to women.

1964 ▪ Geraldine Mock flew solo around the world

On April 17, 1964, German-born aviator Geraldine Mock (1925–) became the first woman to fly solo around the world. Mock took off in a single-engine plane from Port Columbus, Ohio, on March 19, 1964, made 21 stops, and logged 22,858.8 miles before completing the flight.

1964 ▪ Mary Calderone founded Sex Information and Education Council

Dr. Mary Calderone founded the Sex Information and Education Council of the United States (SIECUS). SIECUS provides advice and publications on sex education for teachers, physicians, counselors, religious groups, and schools. From 1953 to 1964 Calderone was the medical director of Planned Parenthood Federation of America.

1965 ▪ Mary Two-Axe Early sought Native Canadian women's rights

Mary Two-Axe Early is a Mohawk Indian from the Caughnawaga reserve in Quebec, Canada. After her husband—he was not of Native American descent—died, she was barred from the home she inherited on the reserve. Clause 12 (1)(b) of the Indian Act gave Indian status to wives and children of Indian men but denied it to Indian women marrying non-Indian men. The children of Indian women who married non-Indian men received "nonstatus" classification as well. As early as 1968 Mohawk wives of non-status husbands organized a group called Indian Rights for Indian Women. Under Early's leadership, this movement began a new stage of Native women's involvement in the fight for equality. Despite organized protests, however, the Canadian government was unresponsive, fearful of provoking the hostility of Native American band leaders. In 1981 the government gave permission to individual Indian bands to request that subsection 12 (1)(b) not apply to them, but the majority of Indian bands failed to do so. Finally in 1985 a law repealed the clause.

1965 ▪ Dickey Chapelle died in combat in Vietnam

Georgette (Dickey) Chapelle (1918–1965) began her career as a war correspondent in the South Pacific during World War II (1939–1945). Fearless and passionately patriotic, she is said to have referred to herself as an "interpreter of violence." During the Hungarian Revolution in 1956 she was captured by the Russians and held prisoner for nearly two months. Chapelle went to Vietnam as a freelance journalist in 1961 with a strong anti-Communist bias. For four years she traveled to and from South Vietnam, writing articles for *National Geographic* and *National Observer* magazines. Chapelle also made speeches throughout the States in defense of American involvement in Vietnam's civil war. On November 4, 1965, she joined a U.S. Marine combat patrol in the jungles near Chu Lai, Vietnam. When a land mine detonated, Chapelle was struck in the throat by shrapnel (metal fragments from bombs, mines, or shells) and killed almost instantly.

1965 ▪ Jane Goodall founded Gombe Stream Research Centre

Jane Goodall (1934–) was born in London, England. In 1960, with the support of anthropologist (one who studies the history and culture of human beings based on remains of past societies) Louis Leakey, she began her long-term study of chimpanzee behavior in Gombe, Tanzania (pronounced tan-zuh-NEE-uh; a country in eastern Africa). After receiving a doctorate from Cambridge University, she founded Gombe Stream Research Centre, which is still in operation, having become the longest-running observational research facility on animals in their natural habitat. Through her work Goodall

Through her research with chimpanzees, Jane Goodall increased the understanding of primate behavior.

increased the understanding of primate behavior. She also made significant contributions to chimpanzee conservation in Africa and to the protection of chimpanzees used in scientific research. Goodall wrote *The Chimpanzee Family Book* (1989) and has published works on wild dogs, jackals, and hyenas. She received the Albert Schweitzer Award in 1987 and the Kyoto Prize for Science in 1990.

1965 ▪ Judy Chicago cofounded Feminist Studio Workshop

Judy Chicago (1939–) was born Judy Cohen in Chicago, Illinois. Taking the name of the city where she grew up, Chicago cofounded the Feminist Studio Workshop in Los Angeles, California, in 1965. The studio later became the Women's Building, an organization devoted to fostering women's art. Chicago published her autobiography, *Through the Flower: My Struggle as a Woman Artist,* in 1975.

1965 ▪ Helen Taussig headed American Heart Association

Helen Brooke Taussig (1898–1986) was born in Cambridge, Massachusetts. After deciding to become a doctor she encountered gender discrimination in medical school. She eventually earned a medical degree from Johns Hopkins University. Staying on at Johns Hopkins, Taussig earned a reputation as an expert on congenital heart disease (defects of the heart that develop before birth). In 1944 Taussig and her colleague Alfred Blalock, a heart surgeon, developed the Blalock-Taussig shunt (a device that diverts blood flow). An artificial artery placed between two blood vessels, the shunt saved the lives of "blue babies" who suffered from insufficient blood circulation to the lungs. In 1961 Taussig was also instrumental in banning the U.S. sale of the drug thalidomide, which caused birth defects. She was awarded the 1964 Medal of Freedom and the 1977 National Medal of Science, and in 1965 she became the first woman to head the American Heart Association.

1965 ▪ Joan Baez established Institute for the Study of Non-Violence

American folksinger and political activist Joan Baez (1941–) was born on Staten Island, New York, the daughter of physicist Albert Baez. During the 1960s she gained fame as a folk singer. Baez was raised a Quaker—Quakers, also called members of the Society of Friends, belong to a Christian sect that promotes justice, peace, and simplicity in living—and became active in peace issues. In 1965 she founded the Institute for the Study of Non-Violence in Carmel, California. Two years later she was put in prison for singing antiwar songs outside a military recruiting center in California. Baez was also the cofounder of Humanitas, the International Human Rights Commission, in 1979.

1965 ▪ Twyla Tharp founded Twyla Tharp Dance Company

American choreographer (dance composer) Twyla Tharp (1942–) was born in Portland, Indiana. She studied dance at

Pomona College, the American Ballet Theater School, and Barnard College. In 1965 she founded the Twyla Tharp Dance Company in New York City. Tharp created dances not only for her own troupe but for other companies and is known as one of the century's most original contemporary choreographers. She was also the choreographer of dance sequences for such films as *Hair* (1979) and *White Nights* (1985). Tharp's autobiography, *Push Comes to Shove,* was published in 1992.

1965 ▪ Maria Callas retired

Opera singer Maria Callas (1923–1977) was born in New York City of Greek immigrant parents. She entered the Athens Conservatory in Athens, Greece, in 1937, making her debut four years later. Appearing in opera halls throughout Europe, Callas soon became known for her *bel canto* roles. (*Bel canto* is a pure and precise vocal technique.) She helped revive seldom performed operas and at the time of her retirement in 1965 was ranked one of the greatest dramatic sopranos of the twentieth century. (Soprano is the name given to the highest singing voice of women.) Over the span of her career Callas sang 40 different roles and recorded 20 operas.

1965 ▪ Patsy Mink elected to U.S. House of Representatives

In 1965 Hawaiian Patsy Mink (1927–) took the oath of office for her first of six consecutive terms as a representative to the U.S. Congress from Hawaii. Mink, who is of Japanese descent, was the first Asian American woman to serve in Congress.

1965 ▪ Margaret Breedlove set women's land speed record

On November 4, 1965, at the Bonneville Salt Flats in Utah, Margaret Laneive "Lee" Breedlove set a women's land speed record of 308.65 miles per hour.

c. 1966 ▪ Rita Rossi Colwell conducted research on cholera

Rita Rossi Colwell (1934–) was born in Beverly, Massachusetts. She earned a bachelor of science degree with distinction in bacteriology from Purdue University in 1956. Although she had been accepted to medical school, she remained at Purdue in order to be with Jack Colwell, a fellow graduate student, whom she married that same year. Rossi Colwell would have continued her studies in bacteriology, but the department chairman informed her that giving a fellowship to a woman would have been a waste of money. Instead she earned a master's degree in genetics and then, in 1961, a Ph.D. from the University of Washington in Seattle. Three years later she joined the faculty at Georgetown University in Washington, D.C.

At Georgetown, Colwell headed a research team that was the first to recognize that the bacterium that causes cholera (a disease affecting the stomach and intestinal tract) grows naturally in estuaries. (An estuary is an arm of the sea at the lower end of a river.) This important breakthrough led to better understanding and treatment of cholera. In 1972 Colwell took a position at the University of Maryland, where she investigated microbes (germs) that pollute sea water. She also became a leader in marine biotechnology (the branch of marine biology that deals with the harvesting of medical, industrial, and seafood products). As a founder and president of the University of Maryland Biotechnology Institute, Colwell continued her work to improve the environment and human health through the scientific study of oceans.

Female Airline Employees Launch Suits

Beginning in 1966 the major U.S. airlines became embroiled in a legal action on the issue of flight attendant hiring practices. (Attendants were all females and were then called stewardesses.) Two years later, on February 3, 1968, the Equal Employment Opportunity Commission (EEOC) ruled that gender was *not* a requirement to be a flight attendant. This ruling allowed the hiring of male flight attendants. Female flight attendants later launched legal complaints against standard airline policy requiring them to quit their jobs when they got married, became pregnant, or reached the age of thirty-two.

1966 ▪ Leontyne Price made opera debut

Leontyne Price (1927–) was born in Laurel, Mississippi. She started singing in her church choir, then studied music at Juilliard in New York City. Price soon became the first African American woman to achieve international acclaim in opera. Her rich soprano voice was primarily associated with

Women in the Boston Marathon

On April 19, 1966, Roberta Gibb Bingay became the first woman to run in the Boston Marathon. She finished ahead of more than half of the 415 men in the race. However, Bingay had to wear a hooded sweatshirt to disguise her appearance because women were not allowed to run in the race. In 1967 Katherine Switzer ran in the Boston Marathon, registered as K. Switzer, and was apprehended by a race official. Published photographs of the official trying to tear Switzer's number off her back created a public outcry. Switzer competed officially in the Boston Marathon when it was finally opened to women in 1972.

the work of Italian composer Guiseppi Verdi. (Soprano is the name given to the highest singing voice of women.) In 1966 she was the first woman to sing the leading role in Samuel Barber's *Antony and Cleopatra,* which had its debut as the first opera performed at the new Metropolitan Opera House at Lincoln Center in New York. Barber created this particular role of Cleopatra specifically for Price.

1966 ▪ Constance Baker Motley appointed U.S. District Court judge

Constance Baker Motley (1921–) was a civil rights lawyer who worked to eliminate state-enforced segregation in the South. During her career Motley successfully argued nine civil rights cases before the U.S. Supreme Court. In 1966 she became the first African American woman appointed judge of the U.S. District Court for the Southern Division of New York City.

1967 ▪ Muriel Siebert bought seat on Stock Exchange

American Muriel Siebert (1932–) was the first woman to own a seat (be allowed to trade) on the New York Stock Exchange. The seat cost $445,000, plus an initiation fee of more than $7,500.

1967 ▪ Dian Fossey began study of gorillas

Dian Fossey (1932–1985) was the first female primatologist (one who studies primates, especially nonhumans such as apes and monkeys) to work successfully with gorillas in the African wild, devoting most of her life to their study. With the sponsorship of archaeologist Louis Leakey, Fossey moved to the African nation of Rwanda in 1967 to pursue her research. There she founded the Karisoke Research Center. Fossey then

shifted her efforts from observation of gorillas to their preservation. She recorded her experiences in the book *Gorillas in the Mist* (1983), which became the basis for a 1988 feature film of the same title starring Sigourney Weaver. In 1985—under somewhat mysterious circumstances—Fossey was found dead at her camp.

Dian Fossey was the first female primatologist to work successfully with gorillas in the African wild.

1968 ▪ Nikki Giovanni published first poetry volume

African American poet Nikki Giovanni (1943–) was born Yolande Cornelia Giovanni, Jr., in Knoxville, Tennessee. Educated at Fisk University, she published her first volume of poetry, *Black Feeling, Black Talk,* in 1968. Giovanni was actively involved with the Black Power movement, which worked to gain equality for African Americans in the 1960s. In 1964 she organized the first Black Arts Festival in Cincinnati, Ohio. Four years later she moved to New York City, where she lived and worked for the next decade, recording albums, writing books of

In 1964 poet Nikki Giovanni organized the first Black Arts Festival in Cincinnati, Ohio.

poetry and essays, and giving speeches. Giovanni received much criticism, including threats on her life in 1984, when she refused to take part in a boycott of South Africa because of its apartheid (racial segregation) policy. In 1989 she was appointed professor of English at Virginia Polytechnic Institute. Five years later she published *Racism 101* (1994), a book of essays. Other works by Giovanni include *Cotton Candy on a Rainy Day* (1978) and *Those Who Ride the Night Winds* (1983).

1968 ▪ Shirley Chisholm elected to U.S. Congress

Groundbreaking African American congressional representative Shirley Anita St. Hill (b. 1924) was born in Brooklyn, New York. After marrying Conrad Chisholm in 1949, she was a teacher and social worker. Chisholm served a term in the New York State Assembly from 1964 to 1968. In 1968 she was elected to the U.S. House of Representatives by the Democratic Party, thus becoming the first African American woman elected to Congress. Chisholm focused her legislative efforts on improving employment, educational opportunities, and living conditions for women, racial minorities, and inner-city residents. In 1972 she ran an unsuccessful campaign for the U.S. presidency. Chisholm's campaign raised national discussion about whether the United States was—or will ever be—ready for a female or an African American president.

1969 ▪ Golda Meir elected prime minister of Israel

Golda Mabovich Meir (1898–1978) born in the Ukraine and raised in the United States. She got married in 1917 and made a commitment to the establishment of a Jewish homeland by moving to Palestine in 1921. By 1929 she was an elected delegate to the World Zionist Congress, and she helped smuggle Jews into Palestine during World War II (1939–1945). As one of the original signers of the 1948 proclamation declaring the independence of Israel, Meir was appointed Israel's minister to Moscow. From 1953 to 1966 she served on the Israeli delegation to the United Nations General Assembly. Meir was elected prime minister of Israel in 1969 after an eight-month retirement from politics. During her time in office, tensions with neighboring Arab states were high and she lost political support. Meir resigned in 1974.

1969 ▪ Sharon Sites sailed from Japan to California

American Sharon Sites sailed her 25-foot sloop 5,000 miles from Yokohama, Japan, to San Diego, California, in 74 days, thus becoming the first woman to sail solo across the Pacific Ocean.

1969 ▪ Audrey McElmury won World Road Racing Championship

Cyclist Audrey McElmury won the Women's World Road Racing Championship in Bruno, Czechoslovakia. With her vic-

National Organization for Women Incorporates

In 1967 the National Organization for Women (NOW) was incorporated in Washington, D.C., with headquarters at 1629 K Street, NW, Suite 500. NOW was founded in June 1966 and held its first convention the following October.

tory, McElmury became the first American—man or woman—to win a world road racing title.

1970 ▪ Feminist Kate Millett published *Sexual Politics*

Kate Millett (1934–) was born in St. Paul, Minnesota. After graduating from Columbia University, she began a career as a sculptor. Millett soon became involved in the feminist movement, however, and in 1970 she published her analysis of sexism in American society. Titled *Sexual Politics: A Surprising Examination of Society's Most Arbitrary Folly* and originally written as a doctoral thesis, Millett's work became a bestseller.

1970 ▪ Dolores Huerta negotiated contract with grape growers

Dolores Fernández Huerta (1930–) was born to Mexican American parents in Dawson, New Mexico, and grew up in Stockton, California. She began her activist career as an advocate for Chicanos (Americans of Mexican descent) in the 1950s with the Community Service Organization (CSO), a Mexican self-help group in California. Turning her attention to the living and working conditions of farm laborers, she joined the Agricultural Workers Association (AWA), through which she met CSO director César Chavez. Dissatisfied with the CSO's unwillingness to form a union with the AWA, Huerta and Chavez founded the National Farm Workers Association in 1962 in Delano, California.

By the late 1960s Huerta had led a successful nationwide boycott (the refusal to buy, use, or deal with) of grapes produced by growers in Delano. Then in 1970 she negotiated a contract between the farm workers and the grape growers, and for the first time table grapes were shipped with the union label. Four years later the union was reorganized as the United

Farm Workers (UFW) and was affiliated with the national labor union known as the AFL-CIO (American Federation of Labor and Congress of Industrial Organizations). Chavez was named president and Huerta was elected the union's first vice president. In 1975 the UFW's efforts led to the drafting of the Agricultural Relations Act, which was then signed by California governor Jerry Brown.

1970 ▪ Germaine Greer published *The Female Eunuch*

Germaine Greer (1939–) was born in Australia and educated at the University of Melbourne and Cambridge University in England. In 1970, while on the faculty of Warwick University, Greer published *The Female Eunuch.* (A eunuch is a term given to a man without testes; it is also used to describe people who are somehow deprived of power.) Depicting marriage as legalized slavery for women, she alleged that women's sexuality was distorted by a male-dominated society. The book was an international success, bringing Greer recognition as a spokesperson for women's rights. In 1979 she was appointed director of the Tulsa (Oklahoma) Center for the Study of Women's Literature. Greer continued her involvement in women's issues, contributing to newspapers and magazines and appearing on various television programs. She has also written *Sex and Destiny: The Politics of Human Fertility* (1984) and *The Change* (1991), a study of women and menopause (the time—usually in the middle-age years—when menstrual periods cease).

1970 ▪ Sally Aw Sian chaired International Press Institute

Sally Aw Sian (1931–), a Chinese journalist, was the first woman to chair the International Press Institute, a position she held in Hong Kong until 1971. She was also the founder and first chair of the Chinese Language Press Institute.

1970 ▪ Jockey Diane Crump rode in Kentucky Derby

Diane Crump (1949–) became the first woman jockey to ride in the Kentucky Derby. (The Kentucky Derby is a thoroughbred horse race, also known as the Run for the Roses, held every year in May at Churchill Downs in Louisville.) The previous year, Crump, who had started as a track exercise rider, rode in a race at Hialeah Race Track in Florida. She was the first woman to compete against men at a pari-mutuel track (a race course where bets are placed).

1970 ▪ Maggie Kuhn founded Gray Panthers

Margaret E. Kuhn (1905–1995) was born in Buffalo, New York, and grew up in Memphis, Tennessee. Although Kuhn had been a lifelong crusader for social justice, it was not until she was forced to retire at age 65 from her job with the Presbyterian Church in New York City that she became truly militant (willing to organize and fight for what she believed was fair). In 1970 Kuhn founded the Gray Panthers. (The name was adapted by the media from the Black Panthers, a radical African American group.) The first organization of its kind in the United States, the Gray Panthers was devoted to fighting ageism (prejudice and discrimination against older people) and to bringing attention to the needs of the elderly in America. The Gray Panthers also formed the Media Watch Task Force, which pressured the National Association of Broadcasters to consider age along with race and sex as an area subject to the television code of ethics.

In 1970 Maggie Kuhn founded the Gray Panthers, an organization devoted to the needs of the elderly in America.

1970 ▪ Pat Palinkas joined professional football team

On August 15, 1970, Pat Palinkas signed with the Orlando Panthers of the Atlantic Coast Professional Football League. As a result she became the first woman to play in a professional football game. Palinkas's assignment was to hold the ball for point-after-touchdown kicks (extra points scored after a touchdown by kicking the ball over the goal post).

1970 ▪ Bella Abzug elected to the U.S. Congress

Bella Savitzky Abzug (1920–) was born in the Bronx, New York. After earning a law degree from Columbia University in New York City in 1944, she spent the next 25 years practicing law as an advocate for civil and human rights. She also campaigned for peace, founding the National Women's Political Caucus in 1961. Abzug was elected to the U.S. House of Representatives in 1971. During her tenure she introduced legislation supporting job programs, welfare, environmental issues, and the State of Israel. She ran unsuccessfully for the U.S. Senate in 1976 and for mayor of New York City the following year. Returning to her law practice in 1980, she continued to be active in political issues. Abzug was inducted into the National Women's Hall of Fame in 1994. *Gender Gap: Bella Abzug's Guide to Political Power for American Women* was published in 1984.

1971 ▪ Researcher Cleo Lancaster studied stomach ulcers

Cleo Lancaster was born in Edgecomb County, North Carolina, the daughter of a truck driver and a cook. After earning a bachelor's degree in biology in 1971, she joined the Upjohn Company in Kalamazoo, Michigan, as a research associate in gastrointestinal (digestive system) research. While at Upjohn, she enrolled in graduate school at Western Michigan University, receiving a master's degree in biomedical science in 1979.

Between 1971 and 1974 Lancaster researched the ulcer-causing effects of nicotine, linking smoking to duodenal (the first part of the small intestine) ulcers in humans. (Ulcers are breaks in mucous membranes.) She has also done work on the effects of ibuprofen versus aspirin and on the ulcer-causing effect of various drugs. In 1991 Lancaster determined that prostaglandins, substances initially found in semen and thought to be produced in the prostate gland, are produced in many parts of the body. (The prostate gland is part of the male sex organ.)

Working with Upjohn colleague André Robert, Lancaster developed two new patents: one for the treatment of pancreatitis (inflammation of the pancreas, which secretes digestive enzymes) and another for the treatment of ulcers. She also helped to develop surgical techniques for the research of gastric secretion.

1971 ▪ Josephine Hulett honored by Afro-American Labor Council

American labor organizer Josephine Hulett (1927–) graduated from the Philadelphia School of Practical Nursing in 1957, but she spent most of her professional life organizing household workers into unions. In 1969 Hulett joined the staff of the National Committee on Household Employment, and from 1969 to 1970 she served as president of Ohio's Youngstown Household Technicians. Two years later she founded the Ohio Coalition of Household Employees. Hulett also served on the Afro-American Labor Council and in 1971 became the first woman to receive its special recognition award.

1971 ▪ Mary Peters Fieser won Garvan Medal

Mary Peters Fieser (b. 1909) was born in Atchison, Kansas. In 1930 she graduated with a bachelor's degree in chemistry from Bryn Mawr College, where she met her future husband, Louis Fieser, a chemistry instructor. When Louis Fieser left Bryn Mawr to teach at Harvard, Mary went with him. At Harvard she performed chemistry research in her future husband's laboratory while earning a master's degree in organic chemistry. When the couple married in 1932, she continued her professional association with her husband on his research team. This arrangement benefitted her enormously in her professional career because discrimination against women in the field of chemistry was very strong at that time.

Fieser was involved in numerous important areas of research, including the synthesis (created by scientists in a lab) of vitamin K, the development of an antimalarial drug (malaria is a disease characterized by chills and fever; it is transmitted by a parasite that reaches the victim's red blood cells through a mosquito bite), and the synthesis of cortisone (a steroid hormone, or chemical messenger, used in the treatment of certain kinds of arthritis) and carcinogenic chemicals for medical research. For her research, publications, and skill in teaching chemistry students how to write, she was awarded the prestigious Garvan Medal in 1971.

1971 ▪ Hannah Weinstein founded Third World Cinema

American film producer Hannah Weinstein (1911–1984) founded Third World Cinema in New York City. This association, with 40 percent of its stock owned by the East Harlem Community Organization, encouraged the creation of films that involved blacks and women in all aspects of production. Among the motion pictures Weinstein made with Third World Cinema were *Claudine* (1972), *Greased Lightning* (1976), and *Stir Crazy* (1980).

1971 ▪ Anne Armstrong co-chaired National Republican Committee

Republican Party leader Anne Legendre Armstrong (1927–) was born in New Orleans, Louisiana, into an old Creole family. (A Creole is a person of European descent born in the West Indies or Spanish America.) After attending Vassar College she served as a volunteer campaigner, then rose through the ranks of the Republican Party. In 1971 Armstrong was appointed co-chair of the National Republican Committee, becoming the first woman to hold this office. She also supported the Equal Rights Amendment, a proposed amendment to the U.S. Constitution that would guarantee equality of rights under the law regardless of sex.

1971 ▪ Erin Pizzey established Chiswick Women's Aid Society

Feminist leader Erin Pizzey (1939–) was born in China and, after the death of her mother, left home at the age of seventeen. Her first marriage—to a broadcaster named Jack Pizzey—ended in 1961. Having moved to England, she founded the Chiswick Women's Aid Society in Chiswick, London, in 1971. Attracting much publicity for her cause, Pizzey became director of Chiswick Family Rescue in 1979. She has also had a career as a writer, publishing books about violence against women, including *Quietly or the Neighbours Will Hear* (1974). In 1982 she and her second husband, Jeff Shapiro, a psychologist, coauthored the controversial study *Prone to Vio-*

lence. Pizzey has also written several novels. After divorcing Shapiro she moved to Italy, where she was awarded the San Valentino d'Oro prize for literature in 1994.

1971 ▪ Billie Jean King won $100,000 in single season

Billie Jean Moffett (1943–) was born in Long Beach, California. In 1965 she married Larry King and also began her career as one of the best players in women's tennis. By 1971 King had become the first female athlete in any sport to earn more than $100,000 in a single season. In 1980 she set another record by winning 20 titles at professional tennis tournaments in Wimbledon, England. King founded *Women's Sports Magazine* in 1974, and she was a cofounder of the Women's Tennis Association. During her tenure as president of the organization she promoted improvement in pay and working conditions for women in professional tennis. In addition to being a television commentator, King has published several books, among them *Secrets of Winning Tennis* (1975) and *Billie Jean King* (1982).

1971 ▪ Jockey Mary Bacon set riding record

On June 30, 1971, jockey Mary Bacon posted her one hundredth victory at the Thistledown Race Track in Cleveland, Ohio, aboard her horse California Lassie. Bacon was the first woman jockey to ride 100 winners.

1971 ▪ Jeanne Holm became U.S. Air Force general

Jeanne Marjorie Holm (1921–) became the first female U.S. Air Force general in 1971. From 1965 until 1972 she served at the Pentagon in Washington, D.C., as director of women in the air force. In 1973 Holm was promoted to major general, the highest rank achieved by any woman in the American armed forces. After retiring in 1974, she founded Women in Government and served as the first chairperson of the organization.

1972 ▪ Ruth Gordon starred in cult film *Harold and Maude*

Ruth Gordon (1896–1985) was born a seaman's daughter in Quincy, Massachusetts. She attended drama school in New

York City and made her Broadway debut in 1918. Early in her career Gordon was told by the American Academy of Dramatic Arts that she was too tiny, too ugly, and too short on talent to be an actress. One critic wrote, "Anyone who looks like that must get off the stage." However, the reviews soon turned positive as she made several impressive performances. With her husband, Garson Kanin, she cowrote the screenplays for the Spencer Tracy-Katherine Hepburn films *Adam's Rib* (1949) and *Pat and Mike* (1952). She received three Oscar nominations for screenwriting. Late in her career Gordon became a cult figure for her performance in the film *Harold and Maude* (1972), the story of a young man who falls in love with an eccentric elderly woman. Gordon also appeared in *Rosemary's Baby* (1968). When she made the film *Maxie* at the age of 87, she insisted on doing her own stunt work and rode a motorcycle for the first time in her life.

Title IX Bans Sex Bias in Education

In 1972 President Richard Nixon signed into law Title IX of the Higher Education Act, which banned sex bias in athletics and other activities at all educational institutions receiving federal assistance.

1972 ▪ Olga Korbut dazzled Olympic audiences

Olga Korbut (1955–) was born in Grodno, Byelorussia. After spending her childhood training as a gymnast, she was chosen for the 1972 Russian Olympic gymnastic team. Competing at the games in Munich, Germany, Korbut dazzled the Olympics audience—as well as millions of television viewers throughout the world—with the agility and grace she demonstrated in a backwards somersault on the uneven parallel bars. She was also the first and only female to do a back flip on the balance beam during these games. Before the 1972 Olympics were over, Korbut had won three gold (first place) medals (a team gold medal, as well as individual gold medals for the beam and floor exercises). She also won a silver (second place) medal for the parallel bars. After retiring from gymnastics in 1976 she turned to coaching. Korbut married Leonid Bartkevich, a pop music star, with whom she had a son.

Gloria Steinem cofounded Ms. magazine, a publication concerned with contemporary feminist issues.

1972 ▪ Gloria Steinem cofounded *Ms.* magazine

Gloria Steinem (1934–) was born in Toledo, Ohio. Through her articles in national publications, her speaking engagements around the country, and various high-profile affiliations, Steinem became a spokesperson and organizer of the women's movement during the 1960s and 1970s. In 1972 she cofounded *Ms.* magazine, a publication on contemporary feminist issues. Steinem's other accomplishments included helping establish the Women's Action Alliance (1970), the National Women's Political Caucus (1971), and the Coalition of Labor Union Women (1974). Her published works include *Outrageous Acts and Everyday Rebellions* (1983) and *Revolution from Within: A Book of Self-Esteem* (1992).

1972 ▪ Judith Jamison named to national arts board

Judith Jamison (1943–) was born in Philadelphia, Pennsylvania. Initially she studied to be a musician, but she later changed her mind and pursued a dancing career. In 1965 she joined the American Dance Theater, which was headed by Alvin Ailey, becoming a soloist for whom Ailey created roles. In 1972 Jamison was the first woman elected to the board of the National Endowment for the Arts (a U.S. government agency that awards grants to arts organizations). She was also the first black artist to serve in this capacity. Jamison was recognized for her wide experience in dance in the United States, Europe, and Africa, as well as for her appearance in the Broadway musical *Sophisticated Ladies* (1981). After working with various dance companies, she returned to the American Dance Theater as artistic director in 1990.

1972 ▪ Juanita Kreps became director of Stock Exchange

American economist Juanita Morris Kreps (1921–) was born in a Kentucky coal-mining town. Her interest in economics resulted from her experience with high unemployment and social problems while growing up. In 1972 Kreps became the first female public director of the New York Stock Exchange (NYSE). She held that position until 1977, when she became the first woman to fill the post of U.S. Secretary of Commerce. Throughout her career Kreps has maintained an interest in economic issues related to age and retirement, the employment of women, and the treatment of racial minorities. Among her published works are *Sex in the Marketplace: American Women at Work* (1971) and *Women and the American Economy* (1976).

1972 ▪ Nina Kuscsik won Women's Boston Marathon

On April 17, 1972, Nina Kuscsik won the women's competition in the Boston Marathon. This was the first time women were permitted to participate in the event held in Boston, Massachusetts, which began in 1896. A native of Long Island, New York, Kuscsik completed the race in three hours, eight minutes, and fifty-eight seconds.

1972 ▪ Bernice Gera umpired professional baseball game

In 1972 Bernice Gera became the first woman to umpire an American professional baseball game. She took the field in a game between minor league teams, the Auburn Phillies and the Geneva Rangers. (A minor league consists of professional baseball teams that do not compete in the major leagues.)

1972 ▪ Patricia Schroeder won seat in U.S. Congress

Patricia Schroeder (1940–) won a seat in the U.S. Congress in 1972. The first woman to represent Colorado,

The Equal Rights Amendment (ERA) Passes U.S. Congress

The Equal Rights Amendment (ERA) was passed by both houses of the U.S. Congress and was signed by President Richard M. Nixon in 1972. It was then sent to the states for ratification. According to the proposed amendment, "Equality of rights under the law shall not be abridged by the United States or by any state on account of sex." In 1982 the amendment expired without being ratified (approved or confirmed) by the required two-thirds of the states, falling just three states short of full ratification.

The U.S. Supreme Court Rules on *Roe v. Wade*

In 1969 attorneys Sarah Weddington and Linda Coffee challenged Texas district attorney Henry Wade over the constitutionality of state abortion statutes that prevented Jane Roe (an alias for Norma McCorvey) from terminating a pregnancy. (At that time all abortions in the state were banned except in cases where a woman's life was endangered by pregnancy.) In Georgia, abortion laws were also challenged in the case of *Doe v. Bolton*. In both cases the Supreme Court decided that in the first trimester (three months) of a pregnancy women have the right to choose an abortion. Since this 1973 Supreme Court decision, pro-life (anti-abortion) and pro-choice (supporters of a woman's right to choose an abortion) movements have waged political, legal, and religious battles over abortion rights and government funding of abortions.

Schroeder entered Congress at a time when few women held such an office. She became an outspoken critic of military spending, and she contributed largely to the passage of the Family and Medical Leave Act. Although Schroeder considered a presidential run in 1988, she found that her gender overshadowed her achievements and consequently decided to back out of the race. Continuing to serve as a representative of Colorado, Schroeder announced her retirement in 1996.

1973 ▪ Dixy Lee Ray headed Atomic Energy Commission

Dixy Lee Ray (1914–1994) was born in Washington State, where she developed a love for the outdoors and a fascination with marine biology (the study of sea creatures). After earning a master's degree from Mills College in 1938, Ray obtained a doctorate in biological science from Stanford University. She then began a 27-year-long career at the University of Washington, where she developed a concern about threats to the environment and the need for greater public understanding of science. In 1973 President Richard Nixon appointed her head of the Atomic Energy Commission. (She was the first woman to hold that position.) Ray went on to a career in politics, becoming the first female governor of the state of Washington in 1976.

1973 ▪ Marcia Frederick won the world gymnastics title

Marcia Frederick became the first American woman to win a world gymnastics title. During the annual World Gymnastics competition, Frederick received a gold (first place) medal for her performance on the uneven parallel bars.

1973 ▪ Shirley Ann Jackson received doctorate

African American scientist Shirley Ann Jackson (1946–) was born in Washington, D.C. Jackson's parents placed a high value on education and supported their daughter's interest in math and science. In 1968 Jackson earned a bachelor's degree from the Massachusetts Institutue of Technology (MIT), followed by a doctorate in 1973. Jackson was the first African American woman to receive a Ph.D. from MIT. Her doctoral thesis concerning elementary particle theory was published in 1975 in *Annals of Physics.* After graduation, Jackson spent many years as a researcher at Bell Laboratories. She was named professor of physics at Rutgers University in 1991.

Shirley Ann Jackson was the first African American woman to receive a doctoral degree from MIT.

1974 ▪ Carla Anderson Hills named U.S. assistant attorney general

In 1974 Carla Anderson Hills (1934–) was appointed assistant attorney general in the Civil Division of the U.S. Department of Justice. She was the first woman to hold this position. The next year President Gerald R. Ford named Hills the U.S. Secretary of Housing and Urban Development (HUD), making her only the third woman in U.S. history to hold a cabinet post. Criticism that a woman was not tough enough to direct the agency was soon quieted: Hills quickly earned a reputation as an efficient, no-nonsense administrator.

1974 ▪ Cecile Hoover Edwards promoted better lives for minorities

Cecile Hoover Edwards (1926–) was born in East St. Louis, Illinois. In 1946 she was awarded a bachelor of science degree with honors from Tuskegee Institute, where she earned a master's degree in chemistry the following year. After completing a doctorate in nutrition at Iowa State University in 1950, she returned to Tuskegee as a faculty member. In 1952

U.S. Women's Professional Football League Founded

A women's professional football league was founded in the United States in 1974. The league included ten teams, all coached by men, and played ten games each year. Every player earned $25 per game.

she became head of Tuskegee's department of foods and nutrition. Among her research studies was the planning of well-balanced and nutritious diets, especially for low-income and disadvantaged populations in the United States and developing countries. Designing a new curriculum for the School of Human Ecology at Howard University was a high point of Edwards's career. She served as dean of the School of Human Ecology from 1972 to 1987.

1974 ▪ Ella Tambussi Grasso elected governor of Connecticut

American congressional representative and governor Ella Tambussi Grasso (1919–1981) was born in Windsor Locks, Connecticut, the daughter of Italian immigrants. In 1974 Grasso was elected governor of Connecticut, thus becoming the first woman in America to win the position in her own right. (Other women had been elected to finish out the terms of their deceased husbands.) When she entered office the state of Connecticut was facing severe financial problems. Taking the challenge, Grasso drafted a strict budget and made cuts in spending. She was ultimately able to balance the budget and produce a surplus in revenues (total income collected for public use). In 1980, while serving her second term, Grasso resigned when she learned she had cancer.

1974 ▪ Julia Miller Phillips produced Oscar-winning film

In 1974 film producer Julia Miller Phillips (1944–) won an Oscar for *The Sting,* which starred Paul Newman and Robert Redford. Phillips was the first woman to win an Academy Award as a producer.

1974 ▪ Barbara Rainey became U.S. Navy pilot

Barbara Rainey (1948–1982) was the first woman to serve as a pilot in the U.S. Navy.

1974 ▪ Isabel Perón became president of Argentina

Isabel Perón (1931–) was born Maria Cartas in La Rioja Province, Argentina. In 1961 she married Juan Perón, who had been removed from office as president of Argentina. The Peróns lived in Spain until 1973, when Juan returned to Argentina to reclaim his presidency. He named Isabel his vice president, and upon his death the following year she succeeded him as president. Isabel Perón thus became the world's first woman president, holding the position until she was ousted during a military coup (overthrow of government) in 1976. Perón was imprisoned by coup leaders on the charge of abusing public property. After her release she moved to Madrid, Spain.

Isabel Perón of Argentina was the world's first female president, a position she held for two years.

1974 ▪ Karen Silkwood died mysteriously

Karen Gay Silkwood (1946–1974) was born in Longview, Texas, and grew up in the heart of oil and gas field country. After an unhappy marriage, Silkwood left her husband and three children and took a job at the Kerr-McGee Cimarron River nuclear facility in Crescent, Oklahoma. The plant manufactured fuel rods used in nuclear fission reactors. (Nuclear fission is the splitting of atomic nuclei; the process emits energy that can be used to power atomic plants and bombs.) Silkwood joined the Oil, Chemical, and Atomic Workers union Local 5-283 and was appointed to a bargaining committee in 1974.

Upon discovering health and safety violations at the Cimarron plant, Silkwood and two other local representatives went to Washington, D.C., to meet with national union leaders and the Atomic Energy Commission. At the meeting, which took place in mid–1974, Silkwood secretly agreed to obtain microscopic photographs of defective fuel rods. Three months later she was driving from Crescent to Oklahoma City to deliver a manila folder containing information about safety violations to a newspaper reporter. Seven miles outside Crescent her car went off the road and plunged over an embankment. Silkwood was killed; the manila folder was not found at the crash site. The circumstances of her death ignited intense controversy about regulation of the nuclear industry. In 1984 the Silkwood story was documented in the movie *Silkwood*, which starred Meryl Streep in the title role.

1975 ▪ Zhengying Qian became water conservation minister

Zhengying Qian (1923–) was one of the first female engineers in China. In 1975 she became the first woman to be appointed minister of water conservation. Seven years later her authority was expanded, and she was the first woman in China to serve as minister of water conservation and power.

1975 ▪ Diana Nyad swam across Lake Ontario

In 1975 Diana Nyad became the first person to swim across Lake Ontario, completing a distance of 32 miles in 20 hours. That year she also swam around Manhattan Island in 7 hours and 57 minutes, thus breaking a record set by Bryon Somers almost a half century earlier. In 1979 Nyad established yet another first in swimming, becoming the first person ever to swim from the Bahamas to Florida.

1976 ▪ Barbara Jordan delivered keynote address

Barbara Jordan (1936–1996) was born in Houston, Texas. She inherited a deep, resonant voice and eloquent speech from her father, who was a Baptist minister, and her mother, who was a noted orator (a skillful public speaker). In 1956, after attending college in Texas, Jordan became the first black student to be admitted to the Boston University Law School. She served six years in the Texas Senate (1966–1972) and was elected to the U.S. House of Representatives. During her six years in Congress, Jordan sponsored bills providing food stamps, emergency housing, and health programs for the poor. Her reputation as one of the twentieth century's great orators was sustained by her keynote address to the 1976 Democratic National Convention. Jordan was the first woman and the first African American to deliver the keynote address. (A keynote address is a speech given to a convention or other assembly to inspire unity and present the issues of primary importance to the group.)

Following her retirement from Congress Jordan joined the faculty at the University of Texas. She was inducted into the National Women's Hall of Fame in 1990, the Texas Women's Hall of Fame in 1984, and the African American Hall of Fame in 1993. She published her autobiography, *Barbara Jordan: A Self-Portrait,* in 1979.

1976 ▪ Susan R. Estrich became president of *Harvard Law Review*

Susan R. Estrich (1952–) was a student at Harvard University Law School when she became the first female president of the *Harvard Law Review.* (Founded in 1887, the *Harvard Law Review* is a prestigious journal that publishes articles about legal issues.) Estrich went on to become the first woman to manage a major U.S. presidential campaign when she headed the campaign of Michael Dukakis, the former governor of Massachusetts, who was the Democratic candidate for the U.S. presidency in 1987. Most recently Estrich has appeared on television as a commentator during televised court trials, including the infamous O. J. Simpson murder case (in which former football great Simpson was accused of murdering his ex-wife, Nicole, and her friend Ron Goldman).

In 1975 Diana Nyad became the first person to swim across Lake Ontario, completing a distance of 32 miles in 20 hours.

1976 ▪ Filmmaker Chantal Akerman gained acclaim

Chantal Akerman (1950–) was born in Brussels, Belgium. She studied film at the INSAS film school of Brussels and the Université Internationale du Théâtre in Paris. In 1976 Akerman gained critical acclaim for her film *Jeanne Dielman.* Akerman, who rejects the label of "feminist," makes films that chronicle the lives of women in a distinct and intimate manner. Her first English-language film, *Histoires d'Amerique* ("American Stories") was released in 1989.

1976 ▪ Judy Rankin became top LPGA money winner

Judy Torluemke Rankin was the first professional female golfer to win more than $100,000 in a single season (1976). Setting this record on the Ladies Professional Golf Association (LPGA) circuit, she went on to earn top money winnings for a second season on the 1977 LPGA tour.

1976 ▪ Krystyna Choynowski-Liskiewicz sailed around the world

On March 28, 1976, Krystyna Choynowski-Liskiewicz of Poland was the first woman to make a solo voyage around the world by sailboat.

1976 ▪ Barbara Walters named TV news anchor

Barbara Walters (1931–) began her television career in 1961 as a writer for the *Today* show, a morning news and entertainment program broadcast on NBC. Eventually she became the *Today* cohost, and in 1974 *Time* magazine named her one of the 200 leaders of the future. In 1976 Walters was the highest-paid TV news personality in history when she joined Harry Reasoner as coanchor (one of two main news readers) of the ABC *Evening News*. She was also the first woman to appear as a coanchor on network television. Famous for her interviews with celebrities, Walters has won several prestigious journalism awards.

1977 ▪ Phyllis Schlafly published anti-feminist book

Phyllis Stewart Schlafly (1924–) was born in St. Louis, Missouri. After graduating from Washington University, she earned a master's degree at Harvard University in 1945, then married Fred Schlafly in 1949. Phyllis Schlafly also obtained a law degree from Niagra University in 1976. A well-known newspaper columnist and television broadcaster, she launched

an extensive campaign in the 1970s against modern feminism. In 1977 Schlafly published *The Power of the Positive Woman* as a statement of her antifeminist views. She also opposed the Equal Rights Amendment (ERA) to the U.S. Constitution. Her "Stop ERA" campaign, with its warnings that the amendment would pave the way for homosexual weddings and women in combat, was largely responsible for the failure of the ERA. Schlafly served on the Commission on the Status of Women from 1975 to 1985, and she was a member of President Ronald Reagan's Defense Policy Advisory Group. She also founded and presided over the Eagle Forum, a national, conservative, pro-family organization.

1977 ▪ Rosalyn Yalow won Nobel Prize

Rosalyn Sussman Yalow (1921–) was born in New York City. The first woman to graduate with a degree in physics from Hunter College (1941), she earned a Ph.D. from the Uni-

In 1977 Rosalyn Yalow (center) received the Nobel Prize for her work on RIA.

versity of Illinois in 1945. Two years earlier she had married Aaron Yalow; the couple later had two children.

While serving as a consultant to the Bronx Veterans Administration (VA) Hospital in New York, she began a collaborating with Solomon Berson on diabetes research in 1950. (Diabetes is a metabolic disorder, so-called because the body cannot break down—or metabolize—carbohydrates properly.) Together they developed the radioimmunoassay (RIA), a method that uses radioactive substances to "label" molecules in the body. In 1977 Yalow received the Nobel Prize for her work on RIA. (Berson died in 1972.) That year she also became the first woman to receive the Albert Lasker Basic Medical Award. From 1973 to 1992 Yalow served as director of the Solomon A. Berson Research Laboratory of the VA Medical Center.

1978 ▪ Helen Thom Edwards began work on Tevatron

Helen Thom Edwards was born in Detroit, Michigan. After graduating with a bachelor's degree from Cornell University in 1957, she remained at the university and completed a doctorate in physics (the science of matter and energy) in 1966. Edwards stayed on as a researcher until 1970, when she became associate head of the Booster Group at Fermi National Accelerator Laboratory. In 1978 Fermilab began work on building a superconducting proton accelerator. (Protons are positively charged particles; an accelerator speeds up the movement of protons.) Edwards was put in charge of designing and building the new accelerator, called the Tevatron. It became the first successful superconducting proton accelerator and was the most powerful accelerator in operation at the end of the twentieth century.

1978 ▪ Jazz musician Toshiko Akiyoshi honored

Toshiko Akiyoshi (1929–) was born in Dairen, China, to Japanese parents. After World War II (1939–1945) she and her family moved to Japan. Although Akiyoshi studied classical music as a teenager, she became interested in jazz during the American occupation of Japan following the war. By 1956, when she was persuaded to move to the United States by American pianist Oscar Peterson, she had already become a well-known musical arranger. For a time Akiyoshi and her first husband, saxophonist Charlie Mariano, led a bebop quartet. (Bebop is a form of jazz.) Becoming increasingly interested in large-scale musical arrangement, Akiyoshi formed the 17-piece Toshiko Akiyoshi Orchestra, which played big-band music with an Asian touch.

During the early 1970s Akiyoshi married saxophone player Lew Tabackin. In 1978 she became the first woman in jazz history to win the *Down Beat* magazine "Best Big Jazz Band" award. She was the subject of the 1982 film documentary *Jazz Is My Native Language,* which describes the effects of her Asian heritage on her uniquely American style of music.

An Underground Feminist Periodical in Russia

Three issues of an underground feminist periodical entitled *Women and Russia: An Almanac to Women about Women* appeared in St. Petersburg (then Leningrad) in 1978. Reporting on the problems of Russian women, the newspaper revealed that females did not enjoy equality with men in the communist system. Such criticism could not be tolerated by the repressive Soviet regime. As a consequence, editor-in-chief Tatyana Mamonova (1943–) and three other women involved with the publication were expelled from the Soviet Union. Articles from *Women and Russia* were published in English in Europe and elsewhere.

1978 ▪ Nina V. Federoff studied cloned maize genes

Nina V. Fedoroff (1942–) was born in Cleveland, Ohio, to Russian immigrants. As a married young mother, Fedoroff entered Syracuse University and began her studies with the aid of a scholarship. She graduated summa cum laude in 1966. For a time she considered becoming a professional musician and was hired as a flutist by the Syracuse Symphony Orchestra. Deciding she could not devote sufficient time to music, Fedoroff returned to school, earned a doctorate in molecular biology from Rockefeller University, and then took a teaching position at the University of California at Los Angeles (UCLA). In the early 1970s Federoff met Barbara McClintock, who would later win a Nobel Prize for her discovery of mobile genes in the chromosomes of corn. Federoff was so intrigued by McClintock's ideas that she studied McClintock's complicated writings on corn chromosomes and educated herself on the subject. Fedoroff left UCLA and joined the Department of Embryology at the Carnegie Institution of Washington, where by 1978 she was placed in a permanent position as a staff scientist. She and her students demonstrated that it was possible to clone maize (Indian corn) genes, which paved the way for further developments in gene cloning. (Cloning is the duplication of an entire organism from a single cell of that organism.) The New York Academy of Sciences named Federoff an outstanding contemporary woman scientist in 1992. (*Also see entry dated 1982: Barbara McClintock won Nobel Prize.*)

1978 ▪ Janet Guthrie placed in the Indianapolis 500

Janet Guthrie (1938–) was born in Iowa City, Iowa. In 1961 she started racing stock cars (a type of racing car) in NASCAR (National Association for Stock Car Auto Racing) competitions and won several awards and races. In 1977 Guthrie became the first woman to qualify for the Indianapolis 500, but her car broke down before she could finish the race. Guthrie entered the Indianapolis race again in 1978, this time finishing in eighth place and becoming the first woman to complete the race. Guthrie's driver's suit and helmet from the 1978 race are on display at the Smithsonian Institution in Washington, D.C. She was elected to the Women's Sports Hall of Fame.

1979 ▪ Jewel Plummer Cobb wrote "Filters for Women in Science"

Jewel Plummer Cobb (1924–) was born in Chicago, Illinois. In 1944 she graduated with a bachelor's degree in biology from Talladega College. After completing a doctoral degree in 1950, Cobb pursued a career as a cell biologist (a scientist who studies the action and interaction of living cells). From 1950 to 1960 she worked at several universities, including New York University and Hunter College in New York. In 1960 she was appointed professor of biology at Sarah Lawrence College, where she continued research on melanoma (or skin cancer) and the ability of melanin (a dark skin pigment) to protect skin from ultraviolet rays. In 1969 Cobb was appointed dean and professor of zoology at Connecticut College. During her tenure at Connecticut she established a privately funded pre-medical graduate program and a pre-dental program for minority students. In 1979 Cobb wrote about the difficulties women face in scientific fields in the essay "Filters for Women in Science," which was published in the book *Expanding the Role of Women in the Sciences*. Two years later she was named president of California State University in Fullerton. She retired in 1990.

1979 ▪ Mother Teresa awarded Nobel Peace Prize

Mother Teresa (1910–) was born Agnes Bojaxhiu in Skopje, Yugoslavia, of Albanian parents. In 1928 she joined the Sisters of Loretto, a Roman Catholic religious order, as a teacher in Calcutta, India. Three years later she took the name of Teresa in honor of Saint Teresa of Ávila, then became a nun in 1937. Mother Teresa left the convent in 1947 to open a school for destitute children in the slums of Calcutta. In 1950 she founded the Order of the Missionaries of Charity, which now has over 200 centers in several countries for the treatment of lepers (people who have contracted the contagious bacterial disease leprosy, which causes muscular degeneration, paralysis, and deformities), the blind, the disabled, the aged, and the dying. In 1979 Mother Teresa was awarded the Nobel Peace Prize for her work.

Boys Town Admits Girls

The first time Boys Town admitted girls was in 1979. Founded in 1917 by Edward J. Flanagan in Omaha, Nebraska, Boys Town is a private, nonsectarian (meaning it is not restricted to a particular religious group) home for homeless, needy, or neglected children. By the mid–1990s it was estimated that more than 8,500 children had received care at Boys Town annually. Sarah Williamson (1975–) was elected the first female mayor of Boys Town in 1991.

Dedication of National Women's Hall of Fame

In 1979 the National Women's Hall of Fame was dedicated at Seneca Falls, New York, the site of the First Woman's Rights Convention in 1848. Twenty-seven women were inducted into the Hall, including Jane Addams (1860–1935), Marian Anderson (1902–1993), Susan B. Anthony (1820–1906), and Clara Barton (1821–1912).

1979 ▪ Beverly Sills named director of New York City Opera

Beverly Sills (1929–) was born Belle Silverman in Brooklyn, New York. She began her career at age three, singing and dancing on a variety of radio programs. Sills made her operatic debut in 1947 and joined the New York City Opera in 1955. For over two decades she performed in opera houses throughout the world. After retiring from the stage in 1979, she became the first female opera singer to be appointed director of the New York City Opera. In 1991 Sills was named managing director of the Metropolitan Opera in New York.

1979 ▪ Margaret Thatcher became British prime minister

Margaret Thatcher (1925–) was born in Lincolnshire, England, the daughter of a grocer and a dressmaker. She and her family lived above the grocery store, and as a young girl she assisted her father in his business. After studying chemistry at Somerville College, Oxford, she married Denis Thatcher in 1951. Following two unsuccessful runs for political office, she earned her law degree in 1953. Six years later Thatcher won a seat in Britain's Parliament, beginning a 20-year career of working for conservative legislation, which included cutting public spending programs in order to strengthen the national economy.

In 1979 Thatcher became Great Britain's first woman prime minister. Her firm economic positions—and her equally firm military stands with the former Soviet Union over Afghanistan and with Argentina over the Falkland Islands—earned Thatcher the title "The Iron Lady." She resigned as prime minister in 1990, having served the longest term of any twentieth-century prime minister. Thatcher published her autobiography, *The Downing Street Years, 1979–1990,* in 1993.

1979 ▪ Ann Meyers signed NBA contract

Ann Meyers signed a one-year contract with the Indiana Pacers in 1979. She was the first woman to play in the National Basketball Association (NBA).

1980 ▪ Nancy D. Fitzroy honored for work in thermal engineering

Nancy Deloye Fitzroy (1927–) was born in Pittsfield, Massachusetts. She studied at Rensselaer Polytechnic Institute in Troy, New York, receiving a bachelor of science degree in chemical engineering in 1949. After working at the Knolls Atomic Power Laboratory and the Hermes Missile Project, she served as a development engineer at General Engineering Laboratory until 1962. During her career Fitzroy was one of the first to study heat transfer surfaces in nuclear-reactor cores, and she holds a patent in the area of cooling of integrated circuits. (Integrated circuits incorporate various electronic components on a single piece of silicon without need for wires.) Fitzroy invented a thermal chip that is used to measure temperatures in such circuits. She also developed a thermal protection system for hardened radar antennae; the system was utilized in the U.S. defense early warning system. Fitzroy received the Society of Women Engineers Achievement Award in 1972 and the Centennial Medallion of the American Society of Mechanical Engineers in 1980.

1980 ▪ Vigdís Finnbogadóttir became president of Iceland

Vigdís Finnbogadóttir (1930–) was born in Reykjavík, Iceland. After being educated in France she returned to Iceland to work for the National Theatre. During the next two decades Finnbogadóttir was actively involved in the cultural life of Reykjavík, teaching art history and drama at the University of Iceland and presenting arts programs on television. In 1980, while she was director of the Reykjavík City Theatre, she was elected president of Iceland. Finnbogadóttir became the first

The Susan B. Anthony One-Dollar Coin

In 1979 the U.S. government issued a one-dollar coin featuring a likeness of suffragist (fighter for women's right to vote) and social reformer Susan B. Anthony, making her the first U.S. woman to have her portrait on a coin in general circulation.

Women's Rights National Historical Park

In 1980 the U.S. Congress passed an act to create the Women's Rights National Historical Park in Seneca Falls, New York, in order to preserve the setting of the First Woman's Rights Convention, which had taken place in 1848. The Declaration Park site features a granite water wall engraved with the text of the Declaration of Sentiments adopted during the 1848 convention. Other preserved sites are the Wesleyan Chapel where the meeting took place and the restored Elizabeth Cady Stanton House. Still standing in the nearby town of Waterloo, New York, is the McClintock House, owned by Quakers Jane and Richard Hunt and rented by Quaker abolitionists Mary Ann and Thomas McClintock. The convention planners met there on July 16, 1848, to draft the Declaration of Sentiments. The Women's Rights National Historical Park is administered by the National Park Service.

woman in history to be elected head of state. She was reelected three times, entering her fourth term in 1992. Having been divorced from her husband since 1963, Finnbogadóttir again made history in 1972 when she became one of the first single persons in Iceland to adopt a child.

1980 ▪ Jeanne Sauvé became speaker of the house in Canada

Jeanne Benoit Sauvé (1922–) was born in Saskatchewan, Canada. After being educated at universities in Canada and Paris she married Maurice Sauvé in 1958. She worked for the United Nations Educational, Scientific, and Cultural Organization (UNESCO) in Paris, France, then was a journalist and broadcaster with the CBC (Canadian Broadcasting Corporation) in Canada. In 1972 Sauvé was elected to Parliament, and in 1980 she became the first woman speaker of the House of Commons in Canada. Acclaimed for her extensive reforms, she was elected governor-general of Canada in 1983.

1981 ▪ Thelma Estrin honored by Society of Women Engineers

Thelma Estrin (1924–) was born in New York City. She received all of her higher education at the University of Wisconsin, earning a bachelor of science degree in 1948, a master of science the following year, and her doctoral degree in electrical engineering in 1951. Estrin has worked hard to further the application of computer technology to neurophysiological research. She developed methods of utilizing the brain's electrical signals—as measured by computers—to study information processing in humans and animals. Her innovations have been refined by other medical researchers and are widely used in the study and diagnosis of brain abnormalities. Estrin received the 1981 Society of Women Engineers Achievement Award.

1981 ▪ Maya Lin designed Vietnam Veterans Memorial

Maya Lin (1959–) was born into an academic and artistic family in Athens, Ohio. Her parents had immigrated to the United States from China. While Lin was an architecture student at Yale University she won the competition to design the Vietnam Veterans War Memorial. Her design featured a black granite wall inscribed with the names of the nearly 58,000 American service personnel who died fighting Vietnam's civil war (1965–1975). Since the memorial was dedicated in 1982 on the Capitol Mall in Washington, D.C., it has become the nation's most popular monument.

First Female Cadets Graduate from West Point

In 1980 the U.S. Military Academy at West Point graduated its first class to include women. The top, or "distinguished," cadets graduated in order of overall performance. Andrea Hollen, a distinguished cadet, was the first of the 63 woman cadets in the class of 1980 to receive her diploma. All received commissions as second lieutenants in the U.S. Army upon graduation from the academy.

c. 1981 ▪ Sylvia A. Earle codesigned "Deep Rover"

Sylvia A. Earle was born in Gibbstown, New Jersey. She received a bachelor of science degree from Florida State University in 1955 and completed a master's degrees in botany at Duke University the following year. In 1970 Earle participated in the Tektite II Project, part of a government-funded study of undersea habitats. She and four other oceanographers lived in an underwater chamber for 14 days off the Bahama Islands. During this time Earle was one of the first researchers to don a mask and oxygen tank and observe the various forms of plant and animal habitats beneath the sea, identifying many new species. Though she set an unbelievable diving record of 1,250 feet, she found serious limitations with a self-contained underwater breathing apparatus (SCUBA gear).

Earle felt that the study of deep-sea marine life would require the assistance of a submersible craft that could dive far

Ocean researcher
Sylvia Earle set an
unbelievable diving
record of 1,250 feet.

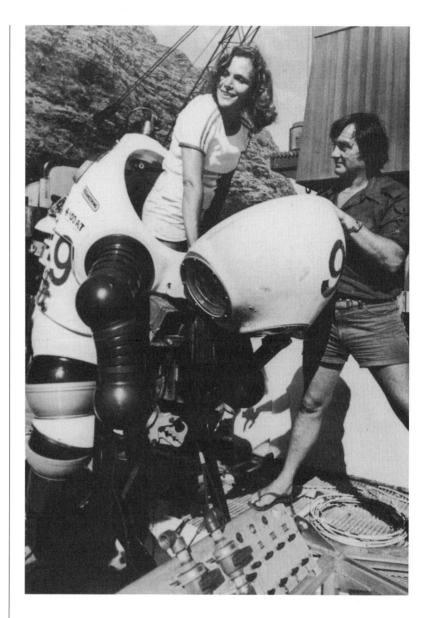

deeper than any person. Earle and her former husband, British-born engineer Graham Hawkes, formed a partnership in 1981 to design and build submersibles. They built "Deep Rover," which continues to operate as a mid-water machine in ocean depths of 3,000 feet. In 1990 Earle was the first woman to serve as chief scientist at the National Oceanic and Atmospheric Administration, the agency that conducts underwater research, manages fisheries, and monitors marine spills. Earle is the coauthor of *Exploring the Deep Frontier: The Adventures of Man in the Sea* (1980).

1981 ▪ Gro Harlem Brundtland elected prime minister of Norway

Gro Harlem Brundtland (1939–) was born in Oslo, Norway. She studied medicine at Oslo and Harvard universities, married politician Arne Olav Brundtland in 1960, and worked in public medical services until 1969, when she entered politics. After being appointed minister of the environment in 1974, Brundtland initiated a program to create nature reserves. Through her support for more liberal abortion laws she also focused attention on the absence of women in Norwegian politics. In 1981 Brundtland was elected prime minister of Norway (a post she held briefly before taking the position again in 1986). The following year she chaired the World Commission on Environment and Development and in 1987 was awarded the Third World Foundation Prize for her work on environmental issues. Although Brundtland lost another election in 1989, she became prime minister again in 1990.

1981 ▪ Jeane Kirkpatrick appointed permanent U.S. representative to United Nations

Jeane Duane Jordan (1926–) was born in Duncan, Oklahoma. After being educated at Columbia University and Paris University, she took a job with the U.S. State Department. In 1955 she married Evron Kirkpatrick, then pursued an academic career, rising to the rank of professor of government at Georgetown University in Washington, D.C., in 1978. Kirkpatrick became well-known as a strong anti-Communist.(Communism is a system of government in which the state controls the means of production and the distribution of goods. It clashes with the American ideal of capitalism, which is based on private ownership and a free market system.) In 1981 she was appointed by President Ronald Reagan as the permanent U.S. representative to the United Nations (UN), a position she held until 1985. (The UN is a world peace organization.) That year she also left the Democratic Party to become a Republican. Published works by

Kirkpatrick include *Political Woman* (1974) and *The Withering Away of the Totalitarian State* (1990).

1981 ▪ Diana Spencer married Charles, the Prince of Wales

Diana Spencer (1961–) was born in Norfolk, England. Educated in England and Sweden, she became a kindergarten teacher in London, England. In 1981 she married Charles, Prince of Wales, the first in line to the British throne. Attended by a congregation of 2,500 and viewed by a worldwide TV audience of 750 million, the royal wedding took place under the dome of St. Paul's Cathedral in London. Subjected to constant public attention and media scrutiny, Diana became increasingly unhappy with the pressures of her role as future queen. In 1992 Buckingham Palace (the headquarters for the royal family) announced that Diana and Charles would live separately. Diana continued to be active as a royal figure, supporting projects for children and victims of AIDS (acquired immunodeficiency syndrome) and serving as an advisor to the International Red Cross. Diana and Charles were officially divorced in 1996. Their eldest son will someday be the king of England.

1981 ▪ Sandra Day O'Connor appointed justice of the U.S. Supreme Court

Sandra Day O'Connor (1930–) was born in El Paso, Texas. Even though she graduated magna cum laude from Stanford Law School, private law firms in the 1950s and 1960s would not hire a woman, so O'Connor went into government and then military service. In 1972 she became Arizona's first female senate majority leader. As a senator O'Connor supported the death penalty and the Equal Rights Amendment. In 1981 she was appointed to the U.S. Supreme Court by President Ronald Reagan. A lifelong moderate or conservative Republican (a believer in maintaining tradition), O'Connor was the first woman to serve on the highest court in the land.

1981 ▪ Janet Young appointed to British ministry post

Janet Young (1926–) was born in Oxford, England. She graduated from Oxford University with a degree in philosophy, politics, and economics. In 1981 Young became the first minister in charge of Great Britain's Management and Personnel Office, responsible for eliminating around 100,000 civil service jobs. In this position she worked to improve job opportunities for women in civil service. In particular, Young strove to prepare more women for top-level positions and fought to make it easier for new mothers to find part-time work.

1982 ▪ Milka Planinc became premier of Yugoslavia

Milka Planinc (1924–) was born in Croatia (a region in the northwestern section of Yugoslavia that was proclaimed an independent state during World War II and became a republic in 1991). She graduated from the Higher Administration in School in Zagreb (the capital city of Croatia) and became party instructor of Zagreb City. In 1957 she served as the political secretary of Treönjevka People's Assembly, and four years later she was named head of the Zagreb secretariat for education and culture. From 1963 to 1965 she served as Republican secretary for education in Croatia. In May 1982 Planinc became president of the Coordination Commission of the Federal Executive Council. She served in that office until 1986.

1982 ▪ Runner Mary Decker set record

Mary Decker Slaney (1958–) was born in New Jersey. Showing early promise as a runner, she was nicknamed the "Golden Girl" and pushed so hard to excel that she suffered several serious injuries throughout her life. From the age of 14 she was forced to undergo numerous operations and spend long periods in plaster casts. In 1982 she ran a mile in under four minutes, becoming the first woman to accomplish this feat. At the World Championships in Helsinki, Finland, the following year, she won gold (first place) medals in the 3,000 meter and 1,500 meter competitions. After divorcing Ron Tabb, a runner, she married Richard Slaney, a British discus thrower. Mary Decker Slaney is perhaps best known for her collision with South African barefooted runner Zola Budd in the 3,000 meter race at the 1984 Olympics in Los Angeles, California. Slaney had to drop out of the race.

1982 ▪ Barbara McClintock won Nobel Prize

Barbara McClintock (1902–1992) was born in Hartford, Connecticut. She received a Ph.D. in botany from Cornell University, where she began her work with maize (Indian corn). Leaving Cornell in 1935, she joined the faculty at the University of Missouri. In 1941 McClintock took a research position at Cold Spring Harbor in New York and continued her maize research. In 1951 at a Cold Spring Harbor symposium she presented her findings on dissociator, or "jumping," genes (a gene that is released from its original position and inserted into a new position). Her work did not receive serious attention, though, until the 1970s. In 1982 McClintock won the Nobel Prize for her discovery of these so-called "jumping" genes. She was the first American woman to win the Nobel Prize in a scientific category by herself. (Previous female winners had shared the honor with other recipients.) McClintock continued her maize research at Cold Spring Harbor until her death in 1992.

1982 ▪ Mildred Cohn won National Medal of Science

Mildred Cohn (b. 1913) was born in New York City to Russian immigrants. In 1931, at age 17, she received a bachelor's degree with honors from Hunter College. But when she entered the doctoral program at Columbia University she learned that teaching assistant positions were awarded only to men. In the meantime Cohn earned a master's degree, then returned to Columbia two years later to seek a doctoral degree. She eventually worked as a researcher at George Washington University Medical School. When her husband joined the physics faculty at Washington University in St. Louis, Missouri, in 1946, Cohn took a position in the school's biochemistry department. She worked with the Nobel Prize-winning husband and wife team of Gerty T. Cori and Carl Ferdinand Cori. She also began pioneering research on enzymes (substances that are produced by living cells and speed up chemical reactions). In 1960 Cohn and her husband moved to the University of Pennsylvania, where Cohn continued her research on enzymes, using nuclear magnetic resonance (NMR). (NMR involves studying the nuclei of chemical elements in a strong magnetic field.) She also studied the reactions of ribonucleic acid (RNA), a key chemical involved in the synthesis (formation) of protein in cells. In 1982 Cohn was awarded the National Medal of Science by President Ronald Reagan.

1983 ▪ Alice Walker awarded Pulitzer Prize

Alice Walker (1944–) was born in Eatonton, Georgia, the youngest of eight children in a family of sharecroppers (tenant farmers who receive a share of the crops they raise). On an income of less than 20 dollars a week, Walker's mother bought her three important gifts: a sewing machine for independence, a suitcase for travel, and a typewriter for writing. Walker graduated valedictorian in high school, attended Spelman College in Georgia on scholarship, and graduated from Sarah Lawrence College in New York in 1965. In 1968 she published her first book, *Once: Poems.* In 1982 Walker published her classic *The Color Purple* (1982), which won the Pulitzer Prize in 1983 and was made into a successful motion picture.

1983 ▪ Ellen Zwilich won prize for music

Ellen Taaffe Zwilich (1939–) was born in Miami, Florida. In 1975, after becoming the first woman to graduate from the Juilliard School of Music, she began a career as a composer. She won numerous awards, including top honors in the International Composition Competition (1975). In 1983 Zwilich became the first woman to win a Pulitzer Prize for music (for her symphony *Three Movements for Orchestra,* a composition commissioned by the American Composers Orchestra).

1983 ▪ Barbra Streisand wrote, directed, produced, and starred in *Yentl*

Barbra Streisand (1942–) was born in Brooklyn, New York. After winning a talent contest as a teenager, she went on to become one of the most famous entertainers in America. By 1968 she was a popular singer, a success on Broadway, and an instant star in the film musical *Funny Girl.* In 1983, with *Yentl,* Streisand also became the first woman to write, direct, produce, and star in a Hollywood movie. In the film she explored the restrictions placed on girls and women in Orthodox Jewish society. Her 1991 venture, *The Prince of Tides,* which she directed, starred in, and coproduced, earned her five Academy Award nominations, including one for best picture. In 1997 Streisand returned to the concert stage in Las Vegas, Nevada, and London, England, for her first live performances in 27 years. That same year she directed *The Mirror Has Two Faces,* which garnered an Academy Award nomination for actress Lauren Bacall.

1983 ▪ Madonna debuted on the pop charts and MTV

Madonna Ciccione (1958–) was born in Rochester, Michigan. Although she studied dancing, she began her professional career as a back-up singer in New York City. In 1983 she released her first solo album, *Madonna,* which contained five hit songs. Among them were "Holiday" and "Burning Up," two cuts that Madonna also recorded as videos, which were played frequently on the music television network MTV. By the late 1980s Madonna had scored 16 consecutive Top 5 hits. The pop diva began her film career in 1985 with *Desperately Seeking Susan.* In 1997 she starred in *Evita,* the film adaptation of the musical stage play about the life of Eva Perón. (*Also see entry dated 1945: Eva Perón supported women's causes in Argentina.*)

1983 ▪ Elizabeth Dole appointed U.S. Secretary of Transportation

Elizabeth Hanford (1936–) was born in Salisbury, North Carolina. In 1975, after becoming a lawyer, she married Robert Dole, then a senator from Kansas. Throughout her career Elizabeth Dole has held several government positions. When she was appointed secretary of transportation in 1983 by President Ronald Reagan, she was only the seventh woman to hold a cabinet position. Dole was responsible for enacting various automobile manufacturing safety rules, requiring that all new cars have air bags or automatic safety belts and rear, eye-level brake lights. She also improved security in airports and hired more federal marshals. In 1990 she was named president of the American Red Cross (an international humanitarian agency). Dole was also active in her husband's unsuccessful campaigns for the U.S. presidency in 1980, 1984, 1992, and 1996.

1983 ▪ Sally Ride became *Challenger* crew member

Sally Kristen Ride (1951–) was born in Los Angeles, California. Although she was a talented tennis player as a teenager, she decided to study physics (the science of matter and energy) in college. After earning a Ph.D. in 1978 Ride was selected for astronaut training with NASA (the National Aeronautics and Space Administration). In June of 1983 she served as a member of the crew of the space shuttle *Challenger*, which traveled in space for six days. The first American woman to travel in space, Ride also designed the shuttle's robot arm (a remote-controlled device that could retrieve items in space). After the *Challenger* flight Ride served as a mission specialist (one who helps plan space flights) for the space shuttle. Since 1989 she has been a professor of physics at the University of California, San Diego.

1983 ▪ Faith Ringgold exhibited story quilt

Faith Ringgold (1930–) was born in the Harlem district of New York City. She started her career as an artist in 1959 when she set up a studio and created traditional paintings, which her second husband, Burdette Ringgold, took to local galleries. Finding that art dealers were reluctant to buy European-style work from an African American woman, Ringgold turned to making story quilts about African American life. These works became her trademark. In 1983 she entered her first quilt in an exhibition. Titled *The Artist and the Quilt,* the piece features faces of people from Ringgold's neighborhood in Harlem. The artist went on to create several other story quilts portraying significant events in African American history. In the 1990s Ringgold also began writing books for children. Her picture book *Tar Beach* (1991) won the Coretta Scott King Illustrator Award and the Caldecott Medal in 1992.

1984 ▪ Prime minister Indira Gandhi assassinated

Indira Gandhi (1917–1984) was born in Allahabad, India, the daughter of Jawaharlal Nehru, the first prime minister of independent India. In 1942 she married Feroze Gandhi, with whom she had two sons. Actively involved in politics, she became a member of the Working Committee of the ruling Congress Parliamentary Party in the 1950s. By 1959 she was president of the party, and in 1966 she was elected prime minister of India as a moderate candidate within the Congress Party.

Gandhi was instrumental in guiding the modernization of India, assisting in the creation of Bangladesh, and establishing India as a nonaligned nation. After she was convicted of election tampering in 1974 she declared a state of emergency, during which civil liberties were restricted and censorship was imposed. When she lost the prime minister post in 1977 she resigned from the Congress Party and formed the Indian National Congress. Elected as prime minister again in 1980, she became embroiled in a Sikh separatist movement. (The Sikhs are members of a religious sect who live mainly in the Punjab region of India.) Gandhi was assassinated by her Sikh security guards in October 1984. Her son Rajiv was also assassinated in 1991, and another son, Sanjay, was killed in an airplane crash in 1980.

1984 ▪ Kathryn Sullivan pioneered satellite refueling

Kathryn D. Sullivan (b. 1951) was the first American woman to participate in extra-vehicular activity in space during a mission in October 1984. Her activity demonstrated the possibility of in-flight satellite refueling.

1984 ▪ Jeanne Sauvé became Canadian governor general

Jeanne Sauvé (1922–) was born in Prud'homme, Saskatchewan, and educated at the University of Ottawa in Canada. Following her marriage in 1948, Sauvé began a distinguished career as a freelance journalist and broadcaster in Montreal. In 1972 she was elected as a liberal Member of Parliament (MP) from Montreal. (Liberals tend to support reform and change in government policy when they feel it is necessary.) On

April 14, 1980, Sauvé became the first woman speaker of the House of Commons, where her extensive reforms earned praise. Four years later Sauvé was sworn in as governor general of Canada, the first woman ever to hold the post.

1984 ▪ Dr. Helene Doris Gayle began career at CDC

Helene Doris Gayle (1955–) was born in Buffalo, New York. She earned a bachelor of arts in psychology in 1976 at Barnard University, followed by a medical degree from the University of Pennsylvania in 1981. After hearing a noted researcher speak on the efforts to eradicate the deadly smallpox virus, Gayle decided to complete a master's degree in public health at Johns Hopkins University in 1981. In 1984 she was accepted to the epidemiology training program at the Centers for Disease Control and Prevention (CDC) in Atlanta, Georgia, where she focused on the AIDS (acquired immunodeficiency syndrome) virus. (Epidemiology is the branch of medical science that deals with the incidence and control of disease in a given population.)

Dr. Helene Doris Gayle views education as a key tool in preventing the spread of AIDS.

Gayle held various positions at the CDC for eight years, concentrating her efforts on the effect of AIDS on children, adolescents, and their families, both in the United States and abroad. In 1992 she joined the AIDS research division of the U.S. Agency for International Development. Three years later she returned to the CDC as director of the office for the prevention of AIDS, other STDs (sexually-transmitted diseases), and tuberculosis (a serious bacterial disease that most often affects the lungs). Gayle views education as a key tool in preventing the spread of AIDS. She has received numerous awards, including the Henrietta and Jacob Lowenburg Prize, the Gordon Miller Award, and the U.S. Public Health Service achievement medal.

Geraldine Ferraro was Walter Mondale's running mate in the 1984 presidential elections.

1984 ▪ Geraldine Ferraro nominated for U.S. vice presidency

Geraldine Ferraro (1935–) was born in Newburgh, New York, the daughter of Italian immigrants. After earning a law degree she married John Zaccaro, a businessman. Ferraro practiced law until 1974, when she joined the district attorney's office in Queens, New York. She then went on to a position with the New York State Supreme Court. In 1981 Ferraro was elected to the U.S. House of Representatives, and in 1984 she was nominated for the U.S. vice presidency.

The first woman ever to be nominated for this office, Ferraro accepted the invitation of Walter Mondale, the Democratic presidential nominee in the 1984 elections. Although Ferraro knew their campaign would not be easy, she was not prepared for the criticism and personal attacks that followed her nomination. Among other charges, she was accused of tax fraud and involvement in organized crime. The Mondale/Ferraro ticket lost in a landslide to President Ronald Reagan, who was elected to his second term as president. Following the campaign Ferraro published *Ferraro, My Story* (1985). She has also written *Changing History: Women, Power, and Politics* (1993). Ferraro was inducted into the Women's Hall of Fame in 1994.

1985 ▪ Margaret Atwood published *The Handmaid's Tale*

Margaret Eleanor Atwood (1939–) was born in Ottawa, Canada, spending part of her childhood in the bush country (a sparsely settled area) of Quebec. After receiving an education in Canada and the United States, Atwood published several collections of poems and short stories. She then turned to writing novels, including *The Edible Woman* (1969) and *Surfacing* (1972). Atwood is perhaps best known for *The Handmaid's Tale* (1985). The novel portrays a vision of the future in which a hostile living environment for women is created by dictatorial fundamentalist Christians (Christians who follow a literal translation of the Bible). In this world environmental pollution has disrupted most women's reproductive capabilities. Women are either Handmaids, the official breeders for society, or men's chattel (slaves). *The Handmaid's Tale* was adapted for film in 1990.

c. 1985 ▪ Lynn Ann Conway helped simplify computer design

Lynn Ann Conway (1938–) was born in Mount Vernon, New York. After receiving a master's degree in electrical engineering from Columbia University in 1963, she worked for several years as a researcher in private industry and at the U.S. Defense Department. In 1985 Conway joined the faculty of the College of Engineering at the University of Michigan, where she gained recognition for two major achievements. First, in a joint effort with several colleagues, she invented a new approach to the design of integrated computer circuit chips. (A computer chip is a tiny piece of silicon, a nonmetal material that conducts electricity. The chip contains integrated circuits, or a large number of electronic components.) Her second major achievement, which was published in the textbook *Introduction to VLSI Systems,* was a new method for making chips, whereby designers could very rapidly obtain models with which to test their hardware (electronic devices) and software (computer program) inventions. Conway's contributions have increased the flow of information to specialized as well as general designers in the computer systems field. She has received extensive recognition for her work, including the John Price Wetherill Medal from the Franklin Institute and the Meritorious Civilian Service Award, both in 1985. Conway was also honored in 1990 with an achievement award from the Society of Women Engineers.

1985 ▪ Libby Riddles won the Iditarod

Libby Riddles (1956–) is an American musher (dogsled driver) who became the first woman to win the Iditarod Trail Sled Dog Race on March 20, 1985. The annual race is a 1,100-mile (1,827-kilometer) marathon from Anchorage to Nome, Alaska.

Wilma Mankiller was the first woman to serve as tribal chief for the Cherokee nation.

1985 ▪ Lynette Woodard played for Harlem Globetrotters

Lynette Woodard (1959–) was a star on the women's basketball team at the University of Kansas. She went on to become the first female player for the legendary Harlem Globetrotters on October 7, 1985. She played her first Globetrotters game in Seattle, Washington, on November 13, 1985.

1985 ▪ Gail Reals became brigadier general

Gail Reals (1937–) was the first woman promoted to the rank of brigadier general in direct competition with men in 1985. Reals served a distinguished career in the U. S. Marine Corps between 1956 and her retirement in 1990.

1985 ▪ Wilma P. Mankiller became chief

Wilma P. Mankiller (1945–) was born in Tahlequah, Oklahoma, the capital of the Cherokee nation of Native American people. Because her family was poor, they sought a better life in California, where Mankiller finished public school and attended college. In 1964 she married Hector Hugo Olaya de Bardi, with whom she had two children. During the late 1960s Mankiller met Native American activists who helped rekindle her own need to serve her people. After divorcing her husband in 1974, she returned to Oklahoma. Using her skills in social work, Mankiller founded the Community Development Department of the Cherokee nation in 1981. Two years later she was elected deputy to Ross Swimmer, the principal chief of the nation. When Swimmer moved on to another position in 1985, Mankiller was sworn in as principal chief. She became the first woman to serve as tribal chief of the Cherokee nation. Between 1985 and her retirement in 1994, Mankiller increased the tribe's membership from 55,000 to 156,000 and added three health centers and nine children's programs to the facilities on Cherokee land.

1986 ▪ Ann Bancroft traveled to North Pole by dogsled

Ann Bancroft (1955–), an American physical education teacher, joined an expedition that set out for the North Pole by dogsled in 1986. The team included five male companions and 21 dogs. After enduring 12-hour days and numerous hardships, they reached the North Pole on May 1, 1986; thus, Bancroft became the first woman to walk to the North Pole.

1986 ▪ Margaret Joan Geller codiscovered "Great Wall"

Margaret Joan Geller (1947–) was born in Ithaca, New York. She received a bachelor's degree from the University of California at Berkeley in 1970 and a doctorate from Princeton University in 1975. Since 1980 Geller has collaborated with astronomer John P. Huchra on a large-scale survey of galaxies. Cosmologists (scientists who study the origin of the universe) have long predicted that galaxies are uniformly distributed in space. Geller and Huchra hypothesized that a three-dimensional mapping of galaxies beyond a certain brightness over a large enough distance—specifically, 500 million light-years—would confirm these predictions of uniformity. (Each light-year is about 6 trillion miles long.)

In 1986 the duo published their first results. Instead of the expected distribution, however, their "slice" of the cosmos showed sheets of galaxies appearing to line the walls of bubble-like empty spaces. Geller and Huchra called this system of thousands of galaxies arranged across the universe the "Great Wall." Geller won a MacArthur fellowship in 1990 for her research and received the Newcome-Cleveland Prize of the American Academy of Arts and Sciences that same year.

1986 ▪ Oprah Winfrey reached national audience

Oprah Winfrey (1954–) was born on a farm near Kosciusko, Mississippi. She participated in the Miss Black America Pageant in 1971, then began her broadcasting career at a television station in Nashville, Tennessee. Moving to Baltimore, Maryland, in 1977, Winfrey was cohost of *Baltimore Is Talking* until 1984, when she took a similar position in Chicago, Illinois. Originally titled A.M. *Chicago,* her program soon became *The Oprah Winfrey Show* and featured audience participation in discussions of controversial issues. By 1986 Winfrey was one of the most famous women in television, each day reaching 17 million viewers who responded enthusiastically to her quick wit and down-to-earth personality.

Winfrey also showed talent as an actress, gaining an Academy Award nomination for her performance in the film *The Color Purple* (1985), which was based on the novel of the same name by Alice Walker. The recipient of numerous other honors for her work in television, she made history as the first woman to own and produce a talk show and the first African American to own a major television studio. Winfrey is also known for her honesty about her weight problems. She published a diet book titled *In the Kitchen with Rosie* (1996), which she put together with her personal cook. In 1997 she premiered an evening television program called *Dinner with Oprah,* in which she talks with writers about literature. Winfrey was inducted into the Women's Hall of Fame in 1994. (*Also see entry dated 1983: Alice Walker won Pulitzer Prize.*)

1986 ▪ Jeana Yeager set nonstop flying record

Jeana Yeager (1952–) grew up in Texas. She was married in 1972 and settled near Houston, but she moved to California five years later after her marriage failed. Pursuing her avid interest in flying, Yeager obtained a pilot's license in 1978. Shortly thereafter she met Dick Rutan, a test pilot, and went to work for the Rutan Aircraft Factory, testing planes designed by Dick's brother Burt. In 1981 Yeager and the Rutans decided to break existing records by designing a plane that would fly around the world with no need for stops or refueling.

Five years and a financial near-disaster later, they finished building the plane, which they named *Voyager.* Yeager and Rutan set out on their flight from Edwards Air Force Base in the Mojave Desert (pronounced mo-HAH-vee) of California on

In 1981 Jeana Yeager decided to design a plane that could fly around the world with no need for stops or refueling.

December 14, 1986. When *Voyager* returned to Edwards Air Force Base on December 23, it had only 10 of its original 1,200 gallons of fuel. They had flown 25,012 miles, more than twice the distance of the previous record set for an unrefueled flight. Yeager and Rutan were presented a medal by President Ronald Reagan, and *Voyager* was placed in the National Air and Space Museum at the Smithsonian Institution in Washington, D.C.

1986 ▪ Corazon Aquino elected president of the Philippines

Corazon (Cory) Aquino (1933–) was born in the Tarlac province of the Philippines, the daughter of a wealthy sugar plantation owner. After receiving an education in New York, she married Benigno Aquino, a politician, in 1956. A leading opponent of Philippine president Ferdinand Marcos, Benigno Aquino was imprisoned for eight years (1972–1980) by the Marcos regime. In 1983 he was assassinated in Manila after

National Museum of Women in the Arts

In 1987 the National Museum of Women in the Arts was established in Washington, D.C. Dedicated to recognizing the achievements of women artists, it is the only museum of its kind in the world.

returning from heart surgery in the United States.

Taking on her husband's mission to fight corruption in government, Aquino defeated Marcos in the 1986 presidential election in the Philippines. One of her first actions as president was to release 441 political prisoners. She also demanded the retirement of generals who had been loyal to the former president. Before a crowd of one million people, Aquino announced that the writ of *habeas corpus* (the right of a prisoner to appear before a judge) was again the law of the land. In addition, she abolished the government's power to imprison people at will, a decree that Marcos had imposed in 1981. Aquino chose not to run for reelection in 1992, instead supporting the successful candidacy of Fidel Ramos.

1986 ▪ Caroline L. Herzenberg collected information on women scientists

Caroline Littlejohn Herzenberg (1932–) was born in East Orange, New Jersey. She received a bachelor of science degree from the Massachusetts Institute of Technology in 1953 and a doctorate from the University of Chicago in 1958. After several years as an academic researcher and teacher, she joined the Argonne National Laboratory, embarking on a long and distinguished career there as a physicist (one who studies the science of matter and energy).

But her contribution to sciences goes beyond research and discovery in the traditional sense. She is probably best known for her work in underscoring the importance of women in science. As president of the Association for Women in Science (1988–1990), she launched an effort to collect biographical information about women who have made advancements in the sciences. Her book, *Women Scientists from Antiquity to the Present* (1986), is one of the most comprehensive listings of women in sciences available and contains a wealth of biographical data. In 1989 Herzenberg was the first woman scientist to be inducted into the Chicago Women's Hall of Fame.

1987 ▪ Gayle Sierens did play-by-play coverage for NFL game

In 1987 Gayle Sierens did play-by-play television coverage of a football game between Kansas City and Seattle. As a result she became the first woman broadcaster to provide commentary for a National Football League (NFL) game.

1988 ▪ Julie Croteau played on men's collegiate basketball team

Julie Croteau took the field for National Collegiate Athletic Association (NCAA) Division III St. Mary's College of Maryland as the first woman to play on a men's collegiate baseball team.

1988 ▪ Benazir Bhutto elected prime minister of Pakistan

Benazir Bhutto (1953–) was born in Karachi, Pakistan. She was educated at Radcliffe College in the United States and at Oxford University in England. Returning to Pakistan in 1977, she became active in politics, opposing the military regime of General Zia ul-Haq. Bhutto was frequently placed under house arrest between 1977 and 1984, when she and her mother Nusrat Bhutto went to England.

While in exile (living outside her native country) Benazir Bhutto became the coleader of the Pakistan People's Party. After martial (military) law was lifted in 1985 she returned to Pakistan to campaign for free elections. In 1987 Bhutto married Asif Ali Zardari, with whom she had two children. Following the death of Zia ul-Haq in 1988, Bhutto was elected prime minister, becoming the first modern-day woman leader of a Muslim nation. Two years later she was removed from office, but she was reelected in 1993. Ousted again in 1996, she made an unsuccessful attempt to regain the post in 1997. Bhutto wrote her autobiography, *Daughter of Destiny,* in 1989.

After being educated at Oxford University, Aung San Suu Kyi became a leader of the National League for Democracy.

1988 ▪ Phyllis Holmes became president of NAIA

On August 1, 1988, Phyllis Holmes became president of the National Association of Intercollegiate Athletics (NAIA). Holmes was the first woman to serve as president of a national coeducational (meaning both sexes participate) sports organization.

1989 ▪ Aung San Suu Kyi placed under house arrest

Aung San Suu Kyi (1946–) was born in Rangoon, Burma (now Yangon, Myanmar). Her father was Aung San, who cofounded the National League for Democracy and headed Burma's fight to gain independence from Great Britain as the country of Myanmar. He was assassinated the year after her birth. After being educated at Oxford University, Aung San Suu Kyi herself became a leader of the National League for Democracy. She left her English husband, Michael Aris, and their two sons in England to return to Burma in 1988. Within a year she was placed under house arrest in her home in Yangon. Her incarceration lasted for 2,190 days, until her release on July 10, 1995. While detained, Suu Kyi became the eighth woman to be awarded the Nobel Peace Prize (1991). She was placed under house arrest again in 1996.

1989 ▪ Katherine Esau won National Medal of Science

Katherine Esau (b. 1898) was born in Ekaterinoslav, Russia. She completed her first year of college before the Russian Revolution led her parents to immigrate to Germany in 1919. Esau was able to complete her bachelor's degree in Germany in 1922 before European political events following World War I (1914–1919) led her parents to move again. The family arrived in the United States in 1922 and settled in California. Esau obtained work with the Spreckels Sugar Company in the agricultural Salinas Valley, where she became a member of the experimental station staff trying to develop a strain of sugar beet resistant to a virus called "curly top." (The disease caused the leafy bloom of the sugar beet plant to wilt, diminishing the size of the valuable white root.)

In 1931 Esau earned her doctoral degree from the University of California at Davis, then joined the faculty there. She conducted research on plant viruses, and that research enabled other scientists to better understand viral damage in specific plant tissues. In addition, she clarified the development phases of plant tissues, particularly the formation of sieve (or strainer-like) tubes which serve to move solutes (dissolved substances) throughout a plant. In 1953 she published *Plant Anatomy,* an important work on plant tissues. Esau received the National Medal of Science in 1989.

1989 ▪ Barbara Harris elected bishop

Barbara Harris (1930–) was born in Philadelphia, Pennsylvania. After working in a variety of jobs during the 1960s she became active in the Episcopal church. In the 1970s she returned to college, receiving theological training at Villanova University. After her ordination as a priest in 1980, she served as a prison chaplain and then as a director of church publications. In 1989 Harris was consecrated assistant bishop of the diocese (district) of Massachusetts, becoming the first woman bishop of the Worldwide Anglican Communion, a 454-year-old organization. Initially the religious community reacted negatively to Harris's appointment because she was a woman holding a position traditionally occupied by men. Within a few months, however, the House of Bishops issued a statement welcoming Harris as a church leader.

1990 ▪ Violeta Chamorro elected president of Nicaragua

Violeta Chamorro (1929–) was born in Rivas, Nicaragua. She attended school in Texas and graduated from Blackstone College in Virginia. Chamorro's political career began in 1979 with the murder of her husband, Pedro Joaquin Chamorro, the editor of *La Prensa* newspaper. He had opposed the regime of Nicaraguan dictator Anastasio Somoza, and his death triggered the 1979 revolution in Nicaragua—a rebellion in which the Sandinistas (members of a revolutionary group who named themselves for another murdered activist, Augusto Sandino) overthrew Somoza.

After briefly supporting the radical Sandinistas, Chamorro used *La Prensa* to organize her own opposition. As a conservative National Opposition Union Party candidate, she was elected president of Nicaragua in 1990, defeating her Sandinista opponent Daniel Ortega. During her presidency Chamorro brought an end to civil war in Nicaragua and initiated constitutional changes that limited presidential power. She left office in 1997, after deciding not to seek reelection.

1990 ▪ Bernadette Locke hired as men's college basketball coach

Bernadette Locke became the first woman to coach a major college men's sport when she accepted the position of assistant coach on the University of Kentucky men's basketball team.

1990 ▪ Mildred S. Dresselhaus won National Medal of Science

Mildred Spiewak Dresselhaus (1930–) was born in Brooklyn, New York. As a child she worked in sweatshops and factories to help with family expenses. The struggling young student managed to graduate from Hunter College with highest honors in 1951, then earned a master's degree in physics (the science of matter and energy) from Radcliffe College in 1953. Soon after receiving a doctorate in physics from the University of Chicago, she married Gene Dresselhaus, a solid state physicist.

In 1960 Dresselhaus joined the staff at Lincoln Laboratory, part of Massachusetts Institute of Technology (MIT), where she studied semimetals (materials such as arsenic and graphite). For her work on the structure of graphite (a form of pure carbon), she received a full professorship at MIT in 1968. Beginning in the 1980s she and her associates investigated the properties of carbon, finding hollow clusters in it, each of which contains 60 atoms.

The challenges Dresselhaus faced as a prominent physicist and mother of four children caused her to become an advocate of women scientists. She worked to expand admissions opportunities for women at MIT, and she began a women's forum to explore solutions to problems faced by working women. As a result of her initiative she was appointed to the Committee on the Education and Employment of Women in Science and Engineering, part of the National Research Council's Commission on Human Resources. In 1990 Dresselhaus was awarded the prestigious National Medal of Science.

1990 ▪ Mary Robinson elected President of Ireland

Mary Bourke Robinson (1944–) was born in Dublin, Ireland. After studying law at Trinity College, Dublin, and at Harvard University, she became an international lawyer. Elected to the Dáil (Irish Parliament) in 1969, she became active in a variety of issues such as women's and homosexuals' rights. A Roman Catholic, Robinson often took positions that opposed the traditional teachings of the Catholic church. In 1990 she was elected president of Ireland, becoming the first woman to hold the office. Her victory occurred during a period of intense controversy over women's rights and abortion. As president Robinson has promoted legislation that enables women to serve on juries and gives 18-year-olds the right to vote. She has also gained respect within the emerging European Community.

1990 ▪ Sandra M. Faber helped identify "great attractor"

Sandra Moore (1944–) was born in Boston, Massachusetts. She obtained a bachelor's degree in physics from Swarthmore College in 1966. While at Swarthmore she met Andrew Leigh Faber, whom she married in 1967. Faber then attended Harvard University, where she completed a doctorate in astronomy in 1972. She later served as an assistant professor and astronomer at the Lick Observatory at the University of California, Santa Cruz. Faber has made significant contributions to our understanding of the big bang theory of the universe (a model of cosmic evolution which states that the universe was created in a giant explosion of a super-dense nucleus of matter some 15 billion years ago).

In 1990, working with a group of six other astronomers, Faber participated in identifying the "great attractor," a concentration of matter whose gravitational pull of galaxies as distant as 150-million light years away seems to defy previously accepted laws of expansion. That same year she helped establish the Keck Observatory on the summit of Mauna Kea in Hawaii, where she is cochair of the science committee. Faber is also a member of the wide-field camera design team for the Hubble Space Telescope.

1990 ▪ Juli Inkster won Spalding Invitational Pro-Am Golf Tournament

In December of 1990 Juli Inkster of Los Altos, California, won the Spalding Invitational Pro-Am Golf Tournament. As a result she became the first woman to win the only professional golf tournament in the world in which women and men compete head-to-head. Inkster parred the eighteenth hole of the Spalding Invitational Pro-Am at Pebble Beach for a one-stroke victory over Professional Golf Association tour member Mark Brooks. ("Par" is the score standard for each hole on a golf course.)

1990 ▪ Adele Goldberg honored for work in computer languages

Adele Goldberg (1945–) was born in Cleveland, Ohio. She received a bachelor's degree in mathematics from the University of Michigan and a master's degree in information sciences from the University of Chicago. Goldberg received her doctorate from the University of Chicago in 1973. She is best known for her work in the 1970s and 1980s with Alan Kay and others in developing the object-oriented computing language called Smalltalk. They also invented a set of programming tools and a user interface (a means of communication between the computer user and computer programs). This interface was the first to use pictures that allowed programmers to interact with overlapping windows on graphical display screens. In 1988 Goldberg cofounded ParcPlace Systems, a company that sells development tools for Smalltalk-based applications. Two years later she received the *PC Magazine* Lifetime Achievement Award. Since 1990 Goldberg has concentrated on issues that help programmers become more effective in using object-oriented technology to solve their computer-related problems.

1991 ▪ Jo Ann Fairbanks refereed international soccer event

In 1991 Jo Ann Fairbanks became the first U.S. female to referee an international soccer event. She served as a lineswoman in the women's qualifying rounds for the North and Central American and Caribbean regional soccer tournament in Haiti.

1991 ▪ Antonia Novello appointed U.S. surgeon general

Antonia Novello (1944–) was born in Fajardo, Puerto Rico. A pre-med student, she received her bachelor's and master's degrees from the University of Puerto Rico. In 1970 Novello began her internship and residency in pediatrics (a branch of medicine concerned with the care of children) at the University of Michigan Medical Center in Ann Arbor. Four years later she joined the staff of Georgetown University Hospital in Washington, D.C., as a pediatric nephrology fellow. (Nephrology is a branch of medicine that deals with the kidneys.) In 1978 and 1979 Novello served as a project officer at the National Institutes of Health's National Institute of Arthritis, Metabolism and Digestive Diseases. Then, in 1989, President George Bush appointed her to the post of U.S. surgeon general. She was the first woman and the first Hispanic to hold this position.

1991 ▪ Judy Sweet elected president of NCAA

In January of 1991 Judy Sweet was elected president of the National Collegiate Athletic Association (NCAA). She was the first woman president of the association.

Blondie Takes a Job Outside the Home

In 1991 the popular comic-strip character "Blondie" took a job outside the home after more than 60 years of homemaking and child rearing. During her first week on the job, she experienced sexual harassment, suffered physical problems from hours of sitting at a computer terminal, and learned that her salary was only 60 percent of that earned by men in her office.

Memorial to U.S. Women Who Died in Vietnam

A memorial to the more than 10,000 women—the majority of them nurses—who died during the U.S. involvement in the Vietnam War was approved by the third and final federal commission authorized to review memorials. The model was designed by Santa Fe, New Mexico-based artist Glenna Goodacre.

1991 ▪ Barbara Hedges named athletic director

In May of 1991 Barbara Hedges was named athletic director for the University of Washington. She was the first female athletic director of a National Collegiate Athletic Association (NCAA) Division I school that included football.

1991 ▪ Sandra Ortiz-Del Valle officiated men's professional basketball game

On July 15, 1991, Sandra Ortiz-Del Valle officiated the United States Basketball League (USBL) game between the New Haven Skyhawks and the Philadelphia Spirit, thus becoming the first woman to officiate a men's professional basketball game.

1991 ▪ Susan Faludi published *Backlash*

Susan Faludi (1960–) was born in Yorktown Heights, New York, and graduated from Harvard University. Beginning her journalism career at the *New York Times,* she later moved to a post with the San Francisco bureau of the *Wall Street Journal.* A committed feminist (fighter for women's rights), Faludi published *Backlash: The Undeclared War on American Women* in 1991. In the book, which became a bestseller, she contends that women are still oppressed within contemporary American society. In 1991 Faludi won both the Pulitzer Prize for investigative journalism and the National Book Critics Circle Award for *Backlash.*

1991 ▪ Bernadine Healy became first female head of NIH

Bernadine Healy (1944–), a cardiovascular (heart) researcher, was appointed by President George Bush to direct the National Institutes of Health in 1991. Healy was the first woman to head the biomedical research facility, which employs 3,200 of America's most prominent medical researchers. After Bill Clinton defeated Bush in the presidential election of 1992, Healy became head of the medical school at Ohio State University.

1991 ▪ Anita Hill testified about sexual harassment

Anita Hill (1956–) was born in Morris, Oklahoma. A graduate of Yale University's law school in 1977, she began private law practice in Washington, D.C. Hill also worked for various U.S. government agencies, including the Equal Employment Opportunity Commission (EEOC), where she was a special assistant to former EEOC director Clarence Thomas. In 1983 she joined the faculty of the University of Oklahoma College of Law.

In 1991 Clarence Thomas was nominated as a U.S. Supreme Court justice by President George Bush. Hill opposed his nomination, accusing him of having sexually harassed her while she worked with him at the EEOC. Pressured by women and the media, the U.S. Senate was forced to reconsider Thomas's candidacy. During nationally televised Senate hearings, Hill gave a graphic description of Thomas's treatment of her. (Thomas denied all of her accusations.) Although Thomas was confirmed by a vote of 52 to 48 in the Senate, Hill's testimony brought about changes in procedures used to evaluate the qualifications of nominees for public office.

1992 ▪ Hanna Suchocka elected Polish prime minister

Hanna Suchocka (1946–) was born in Pleszewa, Poland. In 1968, after she graduated from Poznan University in Poland, Suchocka became a jurist (court lawyer) and a member of the law faculty at the university. From 1980 to 1981 she served as advisor to the Solidarity Trade Union. In 1992 Suchocka became the first woman prime minister of Poland.

"Year of the Women" in American Politics

During the 1992 elections in the United States more women than ever before entered the political arena as office seekers. Between the Democratic and Republican parties, 18 women ran for Senate, 154 for the House of Representatives, 6 for governor, and 3 for lieutenant governor. This record number of female political candidates contributed to 1992 being labeled the "Year of the Women" in American politics.

First Lady Hillary Clinton's outspoken activism has often been the target of sharp criticism.

1992 ▪ Betty Boothroyd became House of Commons speaker

Betty Boothroyd (1929–) was born in Yorkshire, England. After working in a variety of political positions she was elected to the British House of Commons in 1973. Boothroyd became deputy speaker of the House in 1987. When she became a candidate for speaker in 1992, she was elected with bipartisan support (meaning members of both parties supported her), becoming the first woman speaker in the 615-year history of the House of Commons. At the time there were 59 women among the 651 House members.

1992 ▪ Hillary Clinton headed health care commission

Hillary Rodham Clinton (1947–) was born in Park Ridge, Illinois. A graduate of Yale University Law School in New Haven, Connecticut, Clinton made a career as one of America's leading attorneys. In 1975 she married Bill Clinton, who twice served as governor of Arkansas. During his terms as governor, Rodham Clinton chaired a state commission on education and served on corporate and civic boards. During Bill Clinton's successful campaign for the U.S. presidency in 1992, she was his trusted political adviser.

Shortly after the presidential inauguration, Rodham Clinton was appointed chair of a high-level task force charged with producing a nationwide health-care reform plan. Ultimately, however, the task force failed to produce a workable national health-care plan. Rodham Clinton's outspoken activism has often been the target of sharp criticism from the media and from her husband's political opponents—particularly during investigations of alleged wrongdoing by both the president and the first lady. Following Bill Clinton's reelection to office in 1996, Rodham Clinton continued as his advisor and as an active first lady, championing such causes as children's rights.

1992 ▪ Patricia S. Cowings helped reduce motion sickness in astronauts

Patricia Suzanne Cowings (1948–) was born in New York City. She graduated with honors in psychology from the State University of New York at Stony Brook in 1970. Three years later she earned both a master's degree and a doctorate in psychology from the University of California at Davis. After teaching part-time at the University of Nevada, Cowings joined the National Aeronautics and Space Administration (NASA) in 1977 as a research psychologist and principal investigator at the Ames Psychophysiological Research Laboratory in California. (Psychophysiology is a study involving mental and bodily processes.) Cowings then began research on what was called the "zero-gravity sickness syndrome," a condition similar to motion sickness. She was asked to devise a program that might help astronauts minimize their symptoms without drugs. Using biofeedback techniques she conducted experiments with a group of volunteers that resulted in the improvement of their ability to withstand motion sickness. (Biofeedback is a method of consciously controlling various unconscious—or involuntary—bodily processes, such as heart rate and brain waves.) Cowings's work was finally put to use in 1992 during an eight-day flight of the space shuttle *Endeavour.*

In recognition of her contributions as a novelist, Toni Morrison received the Nobel Prize for literature in 1993.

1993 ▪ Toni Morrison awarded Nobel Prize

Toni Morrison (1931–) was born Chloe Anthony Wofford in Lorain, Ohio. She earned degrees from Cornell and Howard universities, returning to Howard to teach in 1957. During this time she changed her name to Toni and she married Harold Morrison, a student from Jamaica with whom she had two sons. After divorcing her husband, Morrison worked as an editor in Syracuse, New York. In 1970 she published her first novel, *The Bluest Eye,* the story of a black girl who wanted blue eyes. She continued exploring the lives of rural African Americans in *Sula* (1974). Morrison won the National Book Critics Circle Award for *Song of Solomon* (1977), and in 1988 she was awarded the Pulitzer Prize in fiction for *Beloved* (1987). In recognition of her contributions as a novelist, Morrison received the Nobel Prize for literature in 1993. She was the first African American to receive this honor.

1993 ▪ Takako Doi became speaker of Lower House

Takako Doi was the first woman to serve as speaker of the Lower House of the Diet, the name given to the Japanese Parliament. During her tenure Doi maintained a reputation as a staunch activist.

1993 ▪ Joycelyn Elders appointed surgeon general

Minnie Joycelyn Elders (1933–) was born in Skaal, Arkansas. She received a medical degree from the University of Arkansas in 1960, joining the faculty as a professor of pediatrics (treatment of children) in 1974. Ten years later she became director of the state's health department. In 1993 Elders was appointed U.S. surgeon general by President Bill Clinton. She became well known for her outspoken views on abortion, AIDS (acquired immunodeficiency syndrome), and drug legalization. The following year Elders was forced to resign from the post for advocating a controversial approach to sex education.

1993 ▪ Janet Reno sworn in as U.S. attorney general

Janet Reno (1938–) was born in Miami, Florida. After earning degrees from Cornell and Harvard universities she began practicing law in 1963. Ten years later Reno became an assistant state attorney in Miami. Then, in 1978, she was elected to the first of four terms as Dade County state attorney. During her tenure she crusaded for children's rights and established the progressive Miami drug court. Reno was also credited with improving relations between law enforcement officials and African American citizens in Dade County.

In 1993 Reno was sworn in as the seventy-eighth attorney general of the United States—the first woman ever to achieve this position. As attorney general, Reno has been straightforward in her politics. She made changes in the nation's crime policy and responded openly to the press and the American people. More recently, Reno has come under fire for her sometimes blunt criticism of White House policy.

1993 ▪ Ruth Bader Ginsburg appointed to U.S. Supreme Court

Ruth Bader (1933–) was born in Brooklyn, New York, the daughter of a clothing store owner. In 1954, while studying at Cornell University, she married Martin Ginsburg, with whom she had two children. When she decided to study for a law degree she encountered discrimination against women at Harvard University, so she transferred to Columbia University, graduating at the top of her class in 1959. She joined the law faculty at Rutgers University in 1963, then returned to Columbia in 1972 as the first tenured female faculty member in the history of the law school. (Tenure is a special status granted to a teacher after satisfactory performance during a trial period.)

Ginsburg was active in the American Civil Liberties Union, and through her work with this group she founded the Women's Rights Project. From 1980 to 1993 she was a circuit court judge with the U.S. Court of Appeals. In 1993 Ginsburg was appointed to the U.S. Supreme Court by President Bill Clinton, becoming the second female justice on the high court and serving with Sandra Day O'Connor, the first female jurist. (*Also see entry dated 1981: Sandra Day O'Connor appointed justice of the U.S. Supreme Court.*)

1993 ▪ Kim Campbell elected prime minister of Canada

Avril Phaedra Campbell (1947–) was born in British Columbia, Canada. When she was 12 she changed her name to Kim. After studying political science at the University of British Columbia and the London School of Economics, she earned a law degree. Campbell practiced law in Vancouver before entering politics. In 1988 she was elected to Parliament, where she opposed a free trade agreement with the

United States. (This agreement was supported by then-Prime Minister Brian Mulroney.) In 1993 Campbell succeeded Mulroney, becoming Canada's first woman prime minister. Later in the year, however, she lost her parliamentary seat in the national election.

1994 ▪ Judith Rodin named president of university

On July 1, 1994, research psychologist Judith Rodin, Ph.D., became the first woman to run an Ivy League school when she took over the presidency of the University of Pennsylvania in Philadelphia. (The "Ivy League" is the term given to eight long-established and highly distinguished colleges in the northeastern United States.)

1995 ▪ Sakhile Nyoni was Botswana's first woman pilot

In 1995 Sakhile Nyoni became the first woman pilot in Botswana, a country in southern Africa. Captain Nyoni flew dignitaries, politicians, and businesspeople on domestic flights throughout Botswana.

1995 ▪ Rebecca E. Marier, valedictorian at West Point

Rebecca E. Marier (1973–) was born in Metairie, Louisiana. In 1995 she graduated at the top of her class at the U.S. Military Academy at West Point, ranking highest in academics and military and physical training. Marier became the first female valedictorian at West Point. She also received the Richard Mason Award, presented to the cadet with highest class standing who had been accepted to medical school.

1995 ▪ Roberta Ramo elected president of American Bar Association

On August 9, 1995, Roberta Cooper Ramo, an attorney from Albuquerque, New Mexico, became the first woman to hold the office of president of the American Bar Association (ABA). As president of the ABA, Ramo strove to improve schoolchildren's knowledge of the U.S. Constitution, to contin-

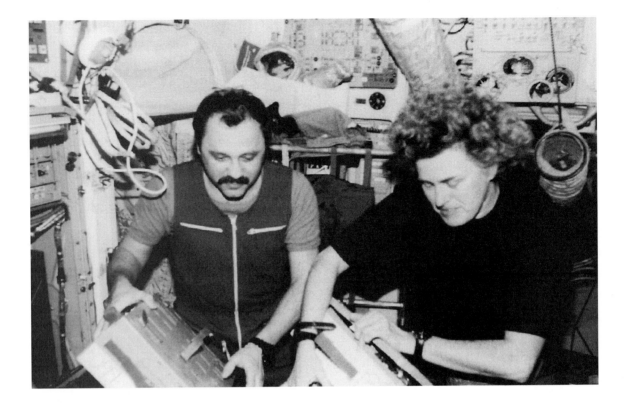

ue financial support for the Legal Services Corporation (which provides legal advice and services for the poor), and to combat domestic violence.

In 1996 astronaut Shannon Lucid traveled aboard the Russian space shuttle Mir for 188 days.

1996 ▪ Shannon Lucid spent longest time in space

Shannon Lucid (1943–) was born in Shanghai, China. After graduating from high school in Bethany, Oklahoma, she attended the University of Oklahoma, where she earned a bachelor's degree in 1963, followed by a medical degree in 1973. In 1978 she became one of the first women selected for the United States National Aeronautics and Space Administration (NASA) space shuttle program. At the time Lucid was a research associate at the Oklahoma Medical Research Foundation in Oklahoma City. Upon becoming an astronaut in 1979, she conducted payload (cargo) testing, shuttle testing, and launch countdown tests.

Lucid took her first space flight in 1985. In 1989, she traveled aboard the orbiter *Atlantis,* which deployed the spacecraft *Galileo* on its exploration voyage to the planet Jupiter. Lucid flew on *Atlantis* again in 1991, making 142 orbits of the earth and logging twenty-one days in space. Her greatest achievement took place in 1996, when she traveled aboard the Russian space shuttle *Mir.* On her 188-day voyage she logged more time in space than any other American astronaut. Lucid was awarded the Congressional Space Medal of Honor by President Bill Clinton in 1996.

1996 ▪ Kerri Strug helped gymnastic team win

Kerri Strug (1977–) was born in Tucson, Arizona. She began training in gymnastics when she was five, following her older brother and sister into gymnastic competition. Fourteen-year-old Strug was the youngest athlete on the U.S. team at the 1992 Olympic games, where she won a bronze medal. During the 1996 Olympics in Atlanta, Georgia, Strug became a heroine when, in spite of a sprained ankle, she executed a dramatic vault to help win a gold medal for the U.S. gymnastics team. This 1996 win represented the first time a U.S. women's gymnastics team had ever won a gold medal in Olympic competition.

1996 ▪ Leni Fischer elected president of assembly

In 1996 Leni Fischer was elected president of the Council of Europe's Parliamentary Assembly. As the Minister of Parliament in Germany, Fischer is the first woman ever to hold the European assembly post.

Index

Bold type indicates main entries
Italic type indicates volume numbers
Illustrations are marked by (ill.)

AARP (see American Association of Retired Persons)

ABA (see American Bar Association)

Abelard *1:* 55

Abolition *1:* 158

Abzug, Bella *2:* **296-297**

Acca Laurentia *1:* **12**

Adams, Hannah *1:* **139**

Adamson, Joy *2:* **275-276,** 276 (ill.)

Aethelflaed *1:* **46**

Agnesi, Maria *1:* **123**

Agrippina the Elder *1:* **22**

Agrippina the Younger *1:* **23,** 24

Akazome Emon *1:* **49**

Akerman, Chantal *2:* **309-310**

Akhmatova, Anna *2:* **219-220,** 220 (ill.)

Akkadian Epic *1:* 1

Albright, Tenley *2:* **264**

Alexiad 1: 57

Allah *1:* 38

Amalasuntha *1:* **35**

Amazons *1:* 9, 14

American Association of Retired Persons (AARP) *2:* 270

American Bar Association (ABA) *2:* 350

American Dance Theater *2:* 302

American Red Cross *2:* 327

American Revolution *1:* 135-136

American Woman Suffrage Association (AWSA): 190

Anderson, Marian *2:* **268**

Andrus, Ethel *2:* **270**

Anguissola, Sofonisba *1:* **89**

Annapurna *2:* 314

Anne of Bohemia *1:* **70**

Anthony, Susan B. *2:* 193, **198,** 317

Antoinette, Marie *1:* **133**

Aphrodite *1:* 5, 13

Aquae Solis *1:* 18

Aquino, Corazon *2:* **335-336**

Arbus, Diane *2:* **274-275**

Arlington, Lizzie *2:* **203**

Armstrong, Anne *2:* **299**

Army nurses *1:* 135

Artemisia I *1:* **15**

Isabel Perón (see entry dated 1974)

Artemisia II *1:* **16**
Astell, Mary *1:* **116-117**
Atanassova, Maria *2:* **269**
Athena *1:* 5, **17-18**
Atilla the Hun *1:* 32-33
Atomic Energy Commission *2:* 304
Atwood, Margaret *2:* **330-331**
Austen, Jane *1:* **150-151**, 151 (ill.)
AWSA (see American Woman
    Suffrage Association)
Ayako, Sono *2:* **266**
Aztecs *1:* 79
Babylon *1:* 5, 6
Bacon, Mary *2:* **300**
Baez, Joan *2:* **287**
Bagley, Sarah *1:* **158-159**
Bagshaw, Elizabeth *2:* **195-196**
Bai, Laskshmi *2:* **184**
Baker, Sara Josephine *2:* **207**,
    207 (ill.)
Ban Zhao *1:* **24**
Bancroft, Ann *2:* **333**
Barbapiccola, Eleanora *1:* **122**
Barbie doll *2:* 273
Barry, Leonora *2:* **198**
Baseball *2:* 203, 233
Basketball: *2:* 204, 274, 317,
    332, 344
Bassi, Laura *1:* **134-135**
Bateman, Hester Needham *1:* **128**
Battle Hymn of the Republic 2: 186
Baudonivia *1:* **39**
Beard, Mary Ritter *2:* **253**
Beasley, Delilah *2:* **228**
Beatrice d'Este *1:* **77-78**
Beaufort, Margaret *1:* **78**
Beecher, Catherine *1:* **154**
Beguine movement *1:* 63, 66
Behn, Aphra *1:* **111**
The Bell Jar 2: 281
Benetton, Giuliana *2:* **267-268**
Berenson, Senda *2:* **204**
Berg, Patty *2:* **244-245**
Bernhardt, Sarah *2:* **189-190**
Beruyah *1:* **27**
Bethune, Mary McLeod *2:* **239**
Bhutto, Benazir *2:* **337-338**
Biographies of Famous Women 1: 18
Birgitta *1:* **69**
Birth control *2:* 195-196, 264
Blackwell, Elizabeth *1:* **168-169**,
    168 (ill.)
Blanche of Castile *1:* **64**
Blankers-Koen, Fanny *2:* **256**

Blodgett, Katherine *2:* **244**, 245 (ill.)
Bloody Mary (see Tudor, Mary)
Bloomer, Amelia *1:* **169**
Bloor, Ella *2:* **211-212**, 212 (ill.)
Bly, Nelly *2:* **198-199**
Bocchi, Dorotea *1:* **71**
Boleyn, Anne *1:* 81, **82-83**, 83 (ill.)
Bonney, Anne *1:* **121-122**
The Book of Margery Kempe 1: 74
Booth, Evangeline *2:* **209**
Boothroyd, Betty *2:* **346**
Born Free 2: 276
Börte *1:* **60**
Boston Marathon *2:* 290, 303
Boudicca *1:* **25-26**, 26 (ill.)
Boulanger, Nadia *2:* **242**
Bourgeois, Louise *1:* **99**
Bourgeoys, Marguerite *1:* **108**
Bourke-White, Margaret *2:* **241**
Boxer Rebellion *2:* 204
Boys Town *2:* 315
Brahe, Sophia *1:* **92**
Brant, Molly *1:* **123**
Breedlove, Margaret *2:* **288**
Breedlove, Sarah *2:* **212**
Bridgman, Laura *1:* **159**
Brontë sisters *1:* **166-167**
Brooke, Charlotte *1:* **140-141**
Brown, Olympia *2:* **188**
Brownell, Kady *2:* **186-187**
Browning, Elizabeth Barrett *1:* **165**
Brundtland, Gro Harlem *2:* **321**
Brunhilda *1:* 36, **37**
Bryant, Helen *2:* **279**
Buddhism *1:* 37-38, 43
Byrd, Mary Willing *1:* **137**
Caccini, Francesca *1:* **97**
Calamity Jane *1:* **199-200**
Calderone, Mary *2:* **284**
Caldwell, Sarah *2:* **269-270**
Callas, Maria *2:* **288**
Campbell, Christiana *1:* **132**
Campbell, Kim *2:* **349-350**
Campfire Girls *2:* 216
Carriera, Rosalba *1:* **121**
Cassat, Mary *1:* **165-166**, 166 (ill.)
Castle, Barbara *2:* **252**
Cathars *1:* 55
Catherine of Aragon *1:* **81-82**, 85
Catherine the Great *1:* **129**,
    129 (ill.)
Catholic Worker 2: 236
"Cattle Raid of Cooley" *1:* 16
Cavendish, Margaret *1:* **108**

Cenci, Beatrice *1:* 95
Chadwick, Florence *2:* 258
Challenger 2: 334
Chamorro, Violeta *2:* 339-340
Champmeslé, Marie *1:* 111-112
Chanel, Coco *2:* 230-231, 231 (ill.)
Chapelle, Dickey *2:* 285
Chattopadhyay, Kamaldevi *2:* 256
Chavez, César *2:* 294-295
Chicago, Judy *2:* 286-
Child, Lydia Maria *1:* 156
Chisholm, Shirley *2:* 292-293
Chudleigh, Elizabeth *1:* 132
Civil War *2:* 186, 187
Claflin, Tennessee *2:* 191-192
Clare of Assisi *1:* 63-64, 64 (ill.)
Claudius *1:* 23, 24, 25
Cleopatra *1:* 19-20, 19 (ill.)
Clinton, Hillary Rodham *2:* 346, 346 (ill.)
Cloelia *1:* 15
Clotild *1:* 34-35, 34 (ill.)
Clovis I *1:* 34-35
Cobb, Jewell *2:* 314-315
Cochran, Jacqueline *2:* 235, 235 (ill.)
Cockacoeske *1:* 113
Cohn, Mildred *2:* 324-325
Colden, Jane *1:* 128
Collette *2:* 204-205, 205 (ill.)
Colonial life *1:* 126
Colonna, Vittoria *1:* 83-84
The Color Purple 2: 325
Colwell, Rita Rossi *2:* 288-289
Coming of Age in Samoa 2: 232
Comnena, Anna *1:* 57
Company of Saint Ursula *1:* 82
Complaint of Ladies 1: 101
Confucius *1:* 87
Connolly, Maureen *2:* 265
Conway, Lynn *2:* 331
Corbin, Hannah Lee *1:* 137-138
Corbin, Molly *1:* 135-136
Corday, Charlotte *1:* 144-145, 144 (ill.)
Cornaro, Elena *1:* 114
Cortés *1:* 79
Countess Loretta *1:* 67-68
Courtly love *1:* 58, 60
Cowings, Patricia S. *2:* 347
Croteau, Julie *2:* 337
Crump, Diane *2:* 295-296
Cult of the Virgins *1:* 52
Cunitz, Maria *1:* 101

Curie, Marie *2:* 208, 208 (ill.)
Dame Trot *1:* 50
Dandridge, Dorothy *2:* 265-266, 266 (ill.)
David-Neel, Alexandra *2:* 229-230, 230 (ill.)
Davis, Margaret B. *2:* 277-278
Davis, Marguerite *2:* 222
Day, Dorothy *2:* 236, 237 (ill.)
de Beauharnais, Josephine *1:* 145-146
de Beauvoir, Simone *2:* 257, 257 (ill.)
De Gouges, Olympe *1:* 141
de Gournay, Marie *1:* 101
de la Cruz, Juana Inés *1:* 115-116
de Marillac, Louise *1:* 102
de Médicis, Catherine *1:* 91-92, 91 (ill.)
de Méricourt, Théroigne *1:* 142-143
De Pisan, Christine *1:* 72
de Rabutin-Chanal, Marie *1:* 112-113
de Scudéry, Madelaine *1:* 97, 104
de Varona, Donna *2:* 284
de Vivonne, Catherine *1:* 94
de Zayas y Sotomayor, Maria *1:* 103
Deborah *1:* 10, 11 (ill.)
Decker, Mary *2:* 323
Déroin, Jeanne *1:* 167-168
Desjardins, Marie-Catherine *1:* 111
Devi *1:* 35
Dhuoda *1:* 45
Dickinson, Emily *2:* 183-184
Didrikson-Zaharias, "Babe" *2:* 234, 234 (ill.)
Discalced Carmelites *1:* 90
DNA *2:* 262
Doe v. Bolton 2: 304
Doi, Takako *2:* 348
Dole, Elizabeth *2:* 326-327
Doña Marina *1:* 79
Double-boiler *1:* 25
Dresselhaus, Mildred S. *2:* 340
Drusilla *1:* 22
du Faur, Emmeline *2:* 217
Duncan, Sara *2:* 197
Durgawati, Maharanee *1:* 90-91
Dyer, Mary Barrett *1:* 109-110
Earhart, Amelia *2:* 235-236
Earle, Sylvia A. *2:* 319-321, 320 (ill.)
Early, Mary Two-Axe *2:* 284-285

Edinger, Tilly *2:* **255-256**
Edwards, Cecile Hoover *2:* **305-306**
Edwards, Helen Thomas *2:* **312**
Elders, Joycelyn *2:* **348**
Eleanor of Aquitaine *1:* **56-57,**
   56 (ill.), 58, 60
Eleanor of Provence *1:* **65-66**
Elion, Gertrude *2:* **277,** 277 (ill.)
Eliot, George *2:* **185**
Elizabeth I *1:* **88-89,** 88 (ill.)
Elizabeth of Hungary *1:* **64-65**
Emma *1:* **52-53**
Empress Adelaide *1:* **50**
Empress Gemmei *1:* **40**
Empress Gensho *1:* **42-43**
Empress Jito *1:* **41-42**
Empress Ma *1:* **68-69**
Empress Matilda *1:* **57-58**
Empress Suiko *1:* 41
Ende *1:* **49**
Enheduanna *1:* **5**
Equal Rights Amendment (ERA)
   2: 303, 311
Equality of Men and Women 1: 101
ERA (see Equal Rights Amendment)
Esau, Katherine *2:* **338-339**
Esther *1:* **16**
Estrich, Susan R. *2:* **309**
Estrin, Thelma *2:* **318-319**
Etruscans *1:* 15
Eurynome *1:* **1-2**
Eustis, Dorothy *2:* **233**
Evans, Elizabeth *2:* **218-219**
Faber, Sandra M. *2:* **341**
Fairbanks, Jo Ann *2:* **343**
Farmer, Fannie *2:* **202**
Farr, Wanda *2:* **231**
Fatima *1:* **38**
Federal Suffrage Association *2:* 188
Federoff, Nina V. *2:* **313-314**
Felicie, Jacqueline *1:* **67**
Felicity *1:* 28
Fell, Margaret Askew *1:* **110**
Ferraro, Geraldine *2:* **330,** 330 (ill.)
Fertility deities *1:* 2
Fields, Dorothy *2:* **243**
Fieser, Mary Peters *2:* **298**
Finnbogadóttir, Vigdís *2:* **317-318**
Fischer, Leni *2:* **352**
Fitzroy, Nancy D. *2:* **317**
Flagstad, Kirsten *2:* **270**
Florentine Academy *1:* 100
Flynn, Elizabeth *2:* **211**
Fontana, Lavinia *1:* **96**

Fonteyn, Margot *2:* **276-277**
Football *2:* 296, 306, 337
Fossey, Dian *2:* **290-291,** 291 (ill.)
Francis of Assisi *1:* 63-64
Franco, Veronica *1:* **94-95**
Frank, Anne *2:* **254,** 254 (ill.)
Frankenstein 1: 153
Franklin, Rosalind *2:* **262**
Franklin, Stella *2:* **206**
Fredegunde *1:* **36-37**
Frederick, Marcia *2:* **304**
Free verse *2:* 223
French Revolution *1:* 141,
   144-145, 157
Freya *1:* 27
Friedan, Betty *2:* **279-280,** 280 (ill.)
Frith, Mary *1:* **99-100**
Fu Hao *1:* **9**
Fuldheim, Dorothy *2:* **255**
Fuller, Margaret *1:* **169-170**
Fuller, Metta *2:* **189**
Fur trade *1:* 109
Gabrielle-Emilie *1:* **125-126**
Gambara, Veronica *1:* **76**
Gandhi, Indira *2:* **328**
Garland, Judy *2:* **248**
Garvan Medal *2:* 298
Gayle, Helene Doris *2:* **329,** 329 (ill.)
Geishas *1:* 95
Geller, Margaret Joan *2:* **333**
Gellhorn, Martha *2:* **251-252**
Genghis Kahn *1:* 60
Genji Monogatari 1: 51
Gentileschi, Artemisia *1:* **100**
Gera, Bernice *2:* **303**
Germain, Sophie *1:* **152-153**
Giblett, Eloise R. *2:* **266-267**
Gibson, Althea *2:* **258,** 259 (ill.)
Giliani, Alessandra *1:* **67**
Ginsberg, Ruth Bader *2:* **349**
Giovanni, Nikki *2:* **291-292,** 292 (ill.)
Girl Scouts *2:* 221-222
Gisela *1:* **52**
Gish, Lillian *2:* **225,** 225 (ill.)
Gladiators *1:* 28
Gleason, Kate *2:* **196-197**
Glückel of Hameln *1:* **105-106**
Goddard, Mary *1:* **134**
Goeppert-Mayer, Maria
   2: **281-282,** 282 (ill.)
Goldberg, Adele *2:* **342**
Golf *2:* 234, 310, 342
Gone with the Wind 2: 241
Goodall, Jane *2:* **285-286,** 286 (ill.)

Gordon, Ruth *2:* 300-301
Gould, Elizabeth *1:* 155
Graham, Bette Nesmith *2:* 269
Graham, Katherine *2:* 279
Grand, Sarah *2:* 202
Grandma Moses (see Moses,
    Anna Mary)
Grasso, Ella *2:* 306
Greek mythology *1:* 5, 9
Greer, Germaine *2:* 295
Grey, Lady Jane *1:* 85, 84 (ill.), 86
Grey Panthers *2:* 296
Grimké, Angelina Emily *1:* 158
Grimké, Sarah Moore *1:* 158
Gripenberg, Alexandra *2:* 197-198
Guanyin *1:* 49
Guggenheim, Peggy *2:* 237-239,
    238 (ill.)
Gulick, Charlotte *2:* 216
Guthrie, Janet *2:* 314
Guy, Alice *2:* 203
Guyart, Marie *1:* 104
Gwyn, Nell *1:* 115
Gymanstics *2:* 301, 304, 352
Haiku poetry *1:* 118
Hale, Sara *1:* 159-160
Halem Globetrotters *2:* 332
The Hammer of Witches 1: 77
Handler, Ruth *2:* 273
Hansberry, Lorraine *2:* 271-272
Hardy, Harriet *2:* 246
Harold and Maude 2: 301
Harper, Frances *2:* 181
Harris, Barbara *2:* 339
Hart, Judith *2:* 272
Harvard Law Review 2: 309
Hathor *1:* 3-4, 4 (ill.), 8
Hatshepsut *1:* 7-8, 7 (ill.)
Haughery, Margaret *2:* 184-185
He Shuangqing *1:* 119
Healy, Bernadine *2:* 344-345
Hedges, Barbara *2:* 344
Heike Monogatari 1: 60
Helen *1:* 10
Helena *1:* 30
Héloïse *1:* 55
Henry II *1:* 56, 58, 60
Henry VIII *1:* 81-82, 83, 85
Hera *1:* 5
Herrad of Landsberg *1:* 59-60
Herschel, Caroline *1:* 140
Herzenberg Caroline L. *2:* 336-337
Hicks, Beatrice *2:* 257-258
Higgins, Marguerite *2:* 260-261

Hilda *1:* 39
Hildegard of Bingen *1:* 58-59
Hill, Anita *2:* 345
Hill, Octavia *2:* 188
Hills, Carla *2:* 305
Himiko *1:* 27
Hindu religion *1:* 35
*History of the Standard Oil
    Company 2:* 209
Hitler, Adolf *2:* 239-240
Hobby, Oveta Culp *2:* 264-265
Hobson, Laura Z. *2:* 255
Hodgkin, Dorothy *2:* 282-283
Hojo Masako *1:* 62
Holiday, Billie *2:* 253, 253
Holm, Jeanne *2:* 300
Holmes, Phyllis *2:* 338
Homer *1:* 9
Hon-Cho-Lo *1:* 95
Hortus deliciarum 1: 59
Howe, Julia Ward *2:* 186
Hrosvitha *1:* 47
Hua Mu-Lan *1:* 32
Huerta, Dolores *2:* 294-295
Huguenots *1:* 91-92
Hulett, Josephine *2:* 298
Hurston, Zora Neale *2:* 243-244
Hutchinson, Anne *1:* 103-104
Hypatia *1:* 31
Ichiko, Kamichika *2:* 258-259
Iditarod *2:* 331
The Illiad 1: 9
Inanna *1:* 5
Inkster, Juli *2:* 342
Inquisition *1:* 64-65
Institute for the Study of
    Nonviolence *2:* 287
International Council of Women
    2: 198
Irene *1:* 43-44, 43 (ill.)
Isabella of Spain *1:* 75-76, 76 (ill.)
Isabelle d'Este *1:* 79-80
Isis *1:* 3, 20
Islam *1:* 38
Italian Renaissance *1:* 94-95
Izumo no Okuni *1:* 95-96
Jackson, Shirley Ann *2:* 305,
    305 (ill.)
Jadwiga *1:* 70-71
Jamison, Judith *2:* 302
Jarvis, Anna *2:* 216
Jesus *1:* 21-22, 30, 52
Jingu *1:* 27
Joan of Arc *1:* 73-74, 73 (ill.)

John of Innsbruck *1:* 68
Johnson, Genora *2:* **242**
Jordan, Barbara *2:* **308-309**
Julian of Norwich *1:* **71-72**
Julius Caesar *1:* 19, 20
Kabuki theater *1:* 95-96
Kaga no Chiyo *1:* **118**
Kagero Nikki 1: 48
Kahlo, Frida *2:* **253-254**
Kakusan Shido *1:* **66**
Kalvak, Helen *2:* **205**
Kamakura Shogunate *1:* 62
Kaminska, Ida *2:* **204**
Kassiane *1:* **44**
Kauffmann, Angelica *1:* **130**
Keller, Helen *2:* **224-225**, 224 (ill.)
Kellerman, Annette *2:* 213 (ill.), **214**
Kempe, Margery *1:* **74**
Kenworthy, Marion *2:* **271**
Khadija *1:* **38**
King, Billie Jean *2:* **300**
Kirkpatrick, Jeane *2:* **321-322**
Knight, Margaret *2:* **191**
Kojiki *1:* **12**, 13, 40
Komer, Odessa *2:* **263**
Komyo *1:* **43**
Koran *1:* 38
Korbut, Olga *2:* **301**
Kreps, Juanita *2:* **302-303**
Kuhn, Maggie *2:* **296**, 296 (ill.)
Kuscsik, Nina *2:* **303**
Kyi, Aung San Suu *2:* **338**, 338 (ill.)
L'Engle, Madeleine *2:* **277**
La Prensa 2: 340
Labé, Louise *1:* **87**
Lady Godiva *1:* **53**
Lady Ise *1:* **46**
Lady Li Fu-jen *1:* **46**
Lagerlöf, Selma *2:* **214**
Lancaster, Cleo *2:* **297**
Lange, Dorothea *2:* **247-248,**
    247 (ill.)
Lavoisier, Antoine *1:* 148-150
Lavoisier, Marie *1:* **148-150,**
    149 (ill.)
Leavitt, Henrietta *2:* **222-223**
Lee, Anna *1:* **136**
Lee, Harper *2:* **275**, 275 (ill.)
Lehmann, Lilli *2:* **193-194**
Letters to the God of Love 1: 72
Lewis, Edmonia *1:* **165**
Leyster, Judith *1:* **99**
Li Qingzhao *1:* **54**

Lilly of the Mowhawks
    (see Tekakwitha, Kateri)
Lin Heier *2:* **204**
Lin, Maya *2:* **319**
Lioba *1:* **42**
The Lion in Winter 1: 57
Littlewood, Joan *2:* **263-264**
Liu Hsiang *1:* **18**
Locke, Bernadette *2:* **340**
Loom and Spindle 1: 157
Louis the Pious *1:* 44-45
Low, Juliette *2:* **221-222**
Lowell, Amy *2:* **223**, 223 (ill.)
Lu Hou *1:* **18**
Lucasta *1:* 24
Lucid, Shannon *2:* **351-352**, 351 (ill.)
Lucretia *1:* **14-15**
Lukens, Rebecca *1:* **154**
Lupercalia *1:* 12
Lyon, Mary *1:* **159**
Macaulay, Catherine *1:* **129-130**
Madame C. J. Walker (see
    Breedlove, Sarah)
Madame de Lafayette *1:* **113-114**
Madame de Rambouillet (see de
    Vivonne, Catherine)
Madame du Barry *1:* **130-131,** 131
Madame du Pompadour *1:* **127**
Madame Roland *1:* **143-144**
Madame Tussaud *1:* **157,** 157 (ill.)
Mademoiselle Maupin *1:* **117-118**
Madonna *2:* **252, 326**
Makeba, Miriam *2:* **271,** 271 (ill.)
Mankiller, Wilma P. *2:* **332,**
    332 (ill.)
Mansfield, Arabella *2:* **190**
Manyoshu 1: 39
Margaret of Austria *1:* **78-79**
Margaret of Tyrol *1:* **68**
Marguerite of Navarre *1:* **81**
Maria the Jewess *1:* **24-25**
Maria Theresa *1:* **125**
Marie d'Oignies *1:* **62-63**
Marie de France *1:* **54-55**
Marie of Champagne *1:* 58, **60**
Marier, Rebecca E. *2:* **350**
Markham, Beryl *2:* **240**
Martha Burke *2:* **199-200,** 199 (ill.)
Martin Luther *1:* 80-81
Mary *1:* **21-22,** 52
Mary I (see Tudor, Mary)
Matilda *1:* **54**
McAuliffe, Christa *2:* 334
McClintock, Barbara *2:* **324**

McCormick, Anne *2:* **242**
McCullers, Carson *2:* **248-249,** 249 (ill.)
McElmury, Audrey *2:* **293-294**
Mead, Margaret *2:* **232,** 232 (ill.)
Meir, Golda *2:* **293**
Mer-Nei *1:* **3**
Merian, Maria Sibylla *1:* **114**
Merici, Angela *1:* **82**
Merit Ptah *1:* **3**
Meyers, Ann *2:* **317**
Miaoshan *1:* **49**
Midwives *1:* 61, 99, 105
Milhaud, Caroline *1:* **146**
Millett, Kate *2:* **294**
Minerva *1:* 18
Ming dynasty *1:* 68-69
Minimum wage *2:* 218-219
Mink, Patsy *2:* **288**
Mins, Donna Mae *2:* **283-284**
Miriam *1:* 8
The Mirror 1: 67
Mitchell, Margaret *2:* **241-242,** 241 (ill.)
Mitchell, Maria *1:* **167,** 167 (ill.)
Mitchell, Verne *2:* **233**
Mock, Geraldine *2:* **284**
Molza, Tarquinia *1:* **92**
Monophysites *1:* 36
Monroe, Marilyn *2:* **262-263,** 263 (ill.)
Montagu, Elizabeth *1:* **131**
Montagu, Mary *1:* **120**
Montessori, Maria *2:* **220-221**
The Montessori Method 2: 220-221
Moodie, Susanna *2:* **182**
Moody, Deborah *1:* **105**
Moody, Helen Willis *2:* **211**
Moore, Marianne *2:* **260,** 260 (ill.)
Morandi, Anna *1:* **128**
Morisot, Berthe *2:* **191**
Morrison, Toni *2:* **347-348,** 347 (ill.)
Moses, Anna Mary *2:* **240**
Mother Teresa *2:* **315**
Mother's Day *2:* 216
Motley, Constance *2:* **290**
Motoko, Hani *2:* **203**
Moulton, Frances *2:* **245-246**
Mount Holyoke Seminary *1:* 159
Ms. 2: 302
Muhammad *1:* 38
Muldowney, Shirley *2:* **272,** 273 (ill.)
Murasaki Shikibu *1:* **51-51**
Murphy, Emily *2:* **226**

Muses *1:* 8
Muslims *1:* 90-91
My Brilliant Career 2: 206
Nakayama Miki *1:* **163**
Nakuta no Okimi *1:* **39**
Napoleonic Code *1:* 145
NASA (See National Aeronautics and Space Administration)
National Aeronautics and Space Administration (NASA) *2:* 351-352
National Dress Reform Association (NDRA) *2:* 183
National Institutes of Health (NIH) *2:* 343, 344
National Medal of Science *2:* 325, 338, 340
National Museum of Women in the Arts *2:* 336
National Organization for Women (NOW) *2:* 293, 294
Nazis *2:* 239-240, 251, 254
NDRA (see National Dress Reform Association)
Nefertari *1:* **6,** 6 (ill.)
Neill, Ann *1:* **138**
Neith *1:* **3-4**
Nerthus *1:* **27**
Nieh Yin-niang *1:* **42**
Nightingale, Florence *2:* **184,** 181 (ill.)
NIH (see National Institutes of Health)
Nihongi 1: 43
No drama *1:* 62
Nobel Prize: *2:* 208, 214, 282, 283, 311, 315, 324, 347
Nogarola, Isotta *1:* **74-75**
Normans *1:* 52-53
Novella d'Andrea *1:* **66**
Novello, Antonia *2:* **343**
NOW (see National Organization for Women)
Nu jie 1: 24
Nur Jahan *1:* **102**
Nureyev, Rudolph *2:* 277
Nyad, Diana *2:* **308,** 309 (ill.)
Nyoni, Sakhile *2:* **350**
Nzinga, Mbande *1:* **100-101**
O'Connor, Flannery *2:* **261**
O'Connor, Sandra Day *2:* **322**
The Odyssey 1: 9
O'Keeffe, Georgia *2:* **228-229,** 229 (ill.)

Oakley, Annie *2:* **197,** 199 (ill.)
Octavia *1:* **25**
Onassis, Jacqueline Kennedy *2:* **278,** 278 (ill.)
Onna Daigaku 1: 117
Order of Poor Clares *1:* 63-64
Order of Saint Savior *1:* 69
Ortiz-Del Valle, Sandra *2:* **344**
Palinkas, Pat *2:* **296**
Pankhurst, Emmeline *2:* **221**
Parker, Dorothy *2:* **225-226**
Parks, Rosa *2:* **268269,** 268 (ill.)
Passion of Saint Perpetua and Felicity 1: 28
Pavlova, Anna *2:* **223-224**
Peck, Annie Smith *2:* **214,** 215 (ill.)
Peeter, Clara *1:* **98**
Pelasgians *1:* 1, 2
Pelletier, Madeleine *2:* **246-247**
Penthesilea *1:* **9-10**
Perkins, Frances *2:* **236**
Perón, Eva *2:* **252**
Perón, Isabel *2:* **307,** 307 (ill.)
Perpetua *1:* **28**
Petrovna, Elizabeth *1:* **127**
Phautasia *1:* **9**
Pickford, Mary *2:* **228**
Pilgrimages *1:* 29
The Pillow Book 1: 51
Pimiku *1:* **28**
Pinckney, Eliza Lucas *1:* **124**
Pinkham, Lydia *2:* **193**
Piracy *1:* 121-122
Pizzey, Erin *2:* **299-300**
Planinc, Milka *2:* **323**
Planned Parenthood *2:* 264
Plath, Sylvia *2:* **280-281**
Pocahontas *1:* **97-98,** 98 (ill.)
Poppaea *1:* 25
Porète, Marguerite *1:* **66-67**
Porter, Sylvia *2:* **250-251**
Preston, Ann *2:* **189**
Price, Leontyne *2:* **289-290**
Princess Olga *1:* **48**
Protestantism *1:* 80-81
Pulitzer Prize *2:* 229, 242, 260, 275, 281, 325
Puritans *1:* 103-104
Qian, Zhengying *2:* **308**
Qin Liangyu *1:* **101**
Qiu Jin *2:* **212-213**
Quant, Mary *2:* **267**
Queen Anne *1:* **118**

Queen Christina *1:* **107**
Queen Elizabeth II *2:* **265**
Queen Isabeau *1:* **73**
Queen Jezebel *1:* **10**
Queen Judith *1:* **44-45**
Queen Liliuokalani *2:* **201-202,** 201 (ill.)
Queen Margrethe *1:* **71**
Queen Medb *1:* **16-17**
Queen of Scots (see Stuart, Mary)
Queen Philippa *1:* **69**
Queen Prabhavata Gupta *1:* **31**
Queen Sammuramat *1:* **11-12**
Queen Tamara *1:* **61**
Queen Theutberga *1:* **45**
Queen Tiy *1:* **8**
Queen Victoria *1:* **160,** 161 (ill.)
Ra *1:* 3, 8
Ragnilda *1:* **49-50**
A Raisin in the Sun 2: 271
Ramo, Roberta *2:* **350-351**
Ranavalona I *1:* **155**
Rankin, Jeannette *2:* **227-228**
Rankin, Judy *2:* **310**
Ratia, Armi *2:* **261**
Ray, Dixie Lee *2:* **304**
Read, Mary *1:* **122**
Reals, Gail *2:* **332**
Reiby, Mary *1:* **152**
Remus *1:* 12
Reno, Janet *2:* **348-349**
Requesta 1: 116
Resnick, Judith *2:* **334**
Revelations 1: 69
Riddles, Libby *2:* **331**
Ride, Sally *2:* **327**
Riefenstahl, Leni *2:* **239-240**
Rind, Clementina *1:* **133**
Ringgold, Faith *2:* **327**
Rivera, Diego *2:* 254
Robinson, Harriet *1:* **157**
Robinson, Mary *2:* **341**
Rodin, Judith *2:* **350**
Roe v. Wade 2: 304
Roldán, Luisa *1:* **116**
Romulus *1:* 12
Ronne, Edith *2:* **254**
Roosevelt, Eleanor *2:* **232-233**
Rose, Ernestine *1:* **162-163**
Ross, Betsy *1:* **136-137**
Rowlandson, Mary *1:* **114-115**
Rubenstein, Helen *2:* **206**
Rudkin, Margaret *2:* **243**

Rudolph, Wilma *2:* **274,** 274 (ill.)
Russian Revolution *2:* 226-227
Ruysch, Rachel *1:* **119**
Sabin, Florence *2:* **206-207**
Sacajawea *1:* **147-148,** 148 (ill.)
Saint Balthild *1:* **40**
Saint Bartholomew's Day
    massacre *1:* 92
Saint Boniface *1:* 42
Saint Brigid *1:* **33**
Saint Catherine *1:* **70**
Saint Catherine *1:* **29-30**
Saint Colette *1:* **72-73**
Saint Genevieve *1:* **32-33**
Saint Mechtilde *1:* **65**
Saint Olympias *1:* **32**
Saint Rose of Lima *1:* **96-97**
Salic Law *1:* 35, 68
Sallé, Marie *1:* **119-120**
Salon society *1:* 94
Salvation Army *2:* 209
Sampson, Deborah *1:* **138-139**
Sand, George *1:* **156,** 156 (ill.)
Sanger, Magaret *2:* **264**
Sano no Chigami *1:* **42**
Sappho *1:* **13-14,** 86
Sati *1:* 47
Sauvé, Jeanne *2:* **318, 328-329**
Schiaparelli, Elsa *2:* **231-232**
Schlafly, Phyllis *2:* **310-311**
Schroeder, Patricia *2:* **303-304**
Schwartz, Sibylle *1:* **104**
Scivias *1:* 59
The Second Sex *2:* 257
Secord, Laura *1:* **151-152**
Sei Shonagon *1:* **51**
Semiramis *1:* **5-6,** 11
Senesh, Hannah *2:* **251**
Seton, Elizabeth *1:* **150**
Sex Information and Education
    Council of the United States
    (SEICUS) *2:* 284
Seymour, Jane *1:* **83,** 85
Sforza, Catherine *1:* **76**
Shakers *1:* 136
Shelly, Mary *1:* **153**
Shinto religion *1:* 12, 28, 37, 39
Shirabyoshi *1:* **62**
Shore, Jane *1:* **75**
Shrine of Ise *1:* 28, 41, 42
Si Ling-shi *1:* **4-5**
Sian, Sally Aw *2:* **295**
Sidney, Mary *1:* 92-93
Siebert, Muriel *2:* **290**

SIECUS (see Sex Information and
    Education Council of the
    United States)
Siege of Calais *1:* 69
Sierens, Gayle *2:* **337**
Silk-making *1:* 3, 4
Sills, Beverly *2:* **316**
Silwood, Karen *2:* **307-308**
Sisters of Charity *1:* 102, 150
Sites, Sharon *2:* **293**
Smallpox *1:* 120
Smith, John *1:* 97
Smith, Margaret Chase *2:* **249-250**
Society of Women Engineers
    2: 257-258
Sonduk *1:* **40**
Song of Deborah *1:* 10
Southern Horrors *2:* 201
Sparta *1:* 14
Spencer, Diana *2:* **322**
Stampa, Gaspara *1:* **86**
Stanton, Elizabeth Cady
    1: **161-162,** 163 (ill.)
Steinem, Gloria *2:* **302,** 302 (ill.)
Stone, Lucy *2:* **190**
Stone, Verlinda *1:* **107**
Stowe, Harriet Beecher *2:* **182-183**
"Street of Crime" *1:* 14
Streisand, Barbara *2:* **325-326**
Strug, Kerry *2:* **352**
Stuart, Mary *1:* **84, 93,** 93 (ill.)
Su Hui *1:* **30**
Su Sanniang *2:* **182**
Suchocka, Hanna *2:* **345**
Suffrage *1:* 137, 138
Suiko *1:* **37**
Sul *1:* **18**
Sullivan, Anne *2:* 224-225
Sullivan, Kathryn D. *2:* **328**
Sun Bu-er *1:* **56**
Sutherland, Joan *2:* **261-261**
Sweet, Judy *2:* **343**
Swimming *2:* 214, 258, 308
The Tale of Genji *1:* 52
Talmud *1:* 27
Tanyangzi *1:* **87**
Taoism *1:* 29, 56
Tarbell, Ida *2:* **209,** 209 (ill.)
Tarquin *1:* 14, 15
Taussig, Helen *2:* **287**
Teerlic, Lavina *1:* **84**
Tekakwitha, Kateri *1:* **112**
ten Boom, Corrie *2:* **250**
Tennis *2:* 211, 258, 265, 300

Tenrikyo religion *1:* 163
Teresa of Avila *1:* **90**
Tereshkova, Valentina *2:* **281**
Tharp, Twyla *2:* **287-288**
Thatcher, Margaret *2:* **316**
*Their Eyes Were Watching
     God 2:* 243
Theodora *1:* **36**
Third World Cinema *2:* 299
Thirty Years' War *1:* 104
Thomas, Clarence *2:* 345
Tiamat *1:* **1**
Title IX *2:* 301
To Kill a Mockingbird 2: 275
Tomoe Gozen *1:* **60-61**
Toshiko, Kishida *2:* **196**
*A Treatise on Divine Providence
     and 26 Prayers 1:* 70
Treaty of Middle Plantation *1:* 113
Treaty of Troyes *1:* 73
Triangle Shirtwaist Fire *2:* 217-218
Trieu Au *1:* **28**
Tristan, Flora *1:* **160-161**
Trojan War *1:* 9, 10
Troubadours *1:* 53
Trung Nhi *1:* **23**
Trung Trac *1:* **23**
Truth, Sojourner *1:* **164**, 164 (ill.);
     2: 193
Tsarina Alexandra *2:* **226-227**
Tuatha Dé Danann *1:* 17
Tubman, Harriet *1:* **170**
Tuchman, Barbara *2:* **281**
Tudor, Mary *1:* **85-86**, 85 (ill.)
Tz'u Hsi *2:* **185-186**, 186 (ill.)
UAW (see United Auto Workers)
Umeko, Tsuda *2:* **205**
UN (see United Nations)
Uncle Tom's Cabin 2: 182-83
United Artists *2:* 228
United Auto Workers (UAW) *2:* 263
United Nations (UN) *2:* 321
Valeria Messalina *1:* **24**, 25
Vestal virgins *1:* 13
Vivien, Renee *2:* **210**
von Bora, Catherine *1:* **80**
**von Greiffenberg, Catherina
     Regina** *1:* **110**
von Grumbach, Argula *1:* **80-81**
von Habsburg, Margaret *1:* **89-90**
von Königsmarck, Maria Aurora
     1: **118**
Walker, Alice *2:* **325**, 334

Walker, Mary Edwards *2:* **187**,
     187 (ill.)
Walsh, Loretta *2:* **227**
Walters, Barbara *2:* **310**
Wang Zhaojung *1:* **20-21**
The Washington Post 2: 279
Waters, Ethel *2:* **247**
WCTU (see Women's Christian
     Temperance Union)
Wei Huacun *1:* **29**
Weinstein, Hannah *2:* **299**
Wells-Barnett, Ida B. *2:* **201**
Wertmuller, Lina *2:* **256-257**
West Point *2:* 319, 350
Wharton, Edith *2:* **229**
"Whirly Girls" *2:* 267
Whitby *1:* 39
Willard, Emma Hart *1:* **153-154**
Willard, Frances *2:* **194-195**
Williams, Shirley *2:* **283**
Winfrey, Oprah *2:* **333-334**
Wise Blood 2: 261
Witchcraft *1:* 77, 96
"Wobblies" *2:* 211
Wollstonecraft, Mary *1:* **143**
Woman's Rights Convention *1:* 164
Women's Aid Society *2:* 299
Women's Christian Temperance
     Union (WCTU) *2:* 195
Women's Hall of Fame *2:* 316
Women's Rights National Historical
     Park *2:* 318
Woodard, Lynette *2:* **332**
Woodhull, Victoria *2:* **191-192**,
     191 (ill.)
World Wildlife Fund *2:* 275
Wright, Frances *1:* **154**
A Wrinkle in Time 2: 277
Wu, Chien-Shiung *2:* **270**
Wu Ze-tian *1:* **41**
Yang Guifei *1:* **43**
Yalow, Rosalyn *2:* **311-312**, 312 (ill.)
Yang Guifei *1:* **43**
Yayoi, Yoshioka *2:* **216-217**
Ye Ziaolan *1:* **102**
Yeager, Jeana *2:* **334-335**, 335 (ill.)
"Year of the Woman" *2:* 345
Yodogimi *1:* **93**
Yoro Code *1:* 43
Young, Janet *2:* **322-323**
Zenobia *1:* **29**
Zwilich, Ellen *2:* **325**